The Companions in Christ Network

www.companionsinchrist.org

So much more!

Companions in Christ is *so much more* than printed resources. It offers an ongoing Leadership Network that provides:

- Opportunities to connect with other small groups who are also journeying through the *Companions in Christ* series.
- Insights and testimonies from other *Companions in Christ* participants
- An online discussion room where you can share or gather information
- Training opportunities that develop and deepen the leadership skills used in formational groups
- Helpful leadership tips and articles as well as updated lists of supplemental resources

Just complete this form and drop it in the mail, and you can enjoy the many benefits available through the *Companions in Christ* Network! Or, enter your contact information at www.companionsinchrist.org/leaders.

Name: ______________________________

Address: ______________________________

City/State/Zip: ______________________________

Church: ______________________________

Email: ______________________________

Phone: ______________________________

Companions in Christ
Upper Room Ministries
PO Box 340012
Nashville, TN 37203-9540

COMPANIONS in Christ
A SMALL-GROUP EXPERIENCE IN SPIRITUAL FORMATION®

The Way of PRAYER

Participant's Book

Jane E. Vennard
with **Stephen D. Bryant**

UPPER ROOM BOOKS®
NASHVILLE

The Way of Prayer Participant's Book
A *Companions in Christ* resource

The Upper Room® Web site: www.upperroom.org

At the time of publication all Web sites referenced in this book were valid. However, due to the fluid nature of the internet some addresses may have changed or the content may no longer be relevant.

Cover design: Left Coast Design, Portland, Oregon
Cover photograph: jupiterimages.com
Icon on back cover flap: "The Pantocrator," image compliments of St. Isaac of Syria Skete, www.skete.com
Second printing: 2008

Library of Congress Cataloging-in-Publication Data

Vennard, Jane E. (Jane Elizabeth), 1940–
Companions in Christ: the way of prayer. Participant's book / Jane E. Vennard & Stephen D. Bryant.
p. cm.
Includes bibliographical references (p. 137).
ISBN-13: 978-0-8358-9906-2
ISBN-10: 0-8358-9906-3
1. Prayer—Christianity. I. Bryant, Stephen D. II. Thompson, Marjorie J., 1953– Companions in Christ. III. Title.
BV215.V45 2007
248.3'2—dc22
200503498 2006023055

Printed in the United States of America

For more information on *Companions in Christ,*
visit www.companionsinchrist.org or call 1-800-972-0433.

Contents

Acknowledgments

The original twenty-eight-week *Companions in Christ* resource grew from the seeds of a vision long held by Stephen D. Bryant, editor and publisher of Upper Room Ministries, and given shape by Marjorie J. Thompson, director of Upper Room's Pathways in Congregational Spirituality and spiritual director to Companions in Christ. The vision, which has now expanded into the Companions in Christ series, was realized through the efforts of many people over many years. The original advisers, consultants, authors, editors, and test churches are acknowledged in the foundational resource. We continue to be grateful to each person and congregation named.

The Way of Prayer is the seventh title in the series building on the foundation of *Companions in Christ*. Like its predecessors, it represents a shorter small-group resource intended to expand on the experience of participation in the twenty-eight-week *Companions* resource. However, a group may use this study prior to experiencing the *Companions in Christ* resource. The articles in the Participant's Book are written by Jane E. Vennard. The daily exercises in the Participant's Book are primarily the work of Stephen D. Bryant and Susanna Southard, based on initial suggestions by Jane Vennard. The Leader's Guide was written by Marjorie Thompson in consultation with Stephen Bryant, Lynne Deming, and Kathleen Stephens. Thanks also to Janet Salyer, Mark Wilson, and Schuyler Bissell for helping us review the material. Other Upper Room staff who worked on this resource include Rita Collett, Janice Neely, and Robin Pippin.

Introduction

Welcome to *Companions in Christ: The Way of Prayer*, a small-group resource designed to help you gain an expanded vision of the nature and practice of prayer, as well as to explore a variety of forms of prayer. Most of us have grown up with a limited understanding of what prayer is, and perhaps an even more limited knowledge of how to pray. Yet there are many ways to pray, both personally and corporately. This resource will help you explore a number of prayer forms through daily practice, so you may discover from experience the expressions of prayer that draw you closer to God and give you a deeper sense of spiritual vitality.

In response to the desire of many small groups to continue exploring spiritual practices that began with the original twenty-eight-week *Companions in Christ* resource, The Upper Room has developed the Companions in Christ series. *The Way of Prayer* is the seventh title in the series. It offers a ten-week journey (plus a preparatory meeting) through an exploration of the nature and practice of prayer. Previous titles in the Companions series include *Exploring the Way*, a six-week introduction to the Christian spiritual journey; *The Way of Grace*, a nine-week journey through central stories in the Gospel of John about encounters with Jesus; *The Way of Blessedness*, a nine-week journey through the Beatitudes; *The Way of Forgiveness*, an eight-week journey through the forgiven and forgiving life; and *The Way of Transforming Discipleship*, a six-week journey plus a Closing Pilgrimage and Retreat through which we hope to experience more deeply what it means to live as a Christ-follower.

With the exception of *Exploring the Way*, each resource in the Companions series expands the foundational content of the original twenty-eight-week resource and uses the same basic format. *Companions in Christ* explored the Christian spiritual life under five headings: Journey, Scripture, Prayer, Call, and Spiritual Guidance. Each supplementary volume explores in greater depth some aspect of one of these five areas of spiritual life and practice. *The Way of Prayer* naturally falls under the general heading of Prayer. It will echo and substantially amplify some of the perspectives and practices introduced in the foundational *Companions* resource.

As people of prayer, our journeys always remain rooted in a biblical understanding of our faith. When we ponder scripture in a *Companions* group, we engage the stories and passages as much as possible with our whole self. We want to include intellect, feeling, intuition, and will as we draw on classic practices of scriptural meditation and prayer. It is important to understand that *Companions* does not offer Bible study in any traditional sense. It represents a more experiential, formational approach to scripture than an informational approach.

Like the original *Companions in Christ* resource, *The Way of Prayer* will help you deepen essential practices of the Christian life. It focuses on your daily experience of God and your growing capacity to respond to grace with gratitude, trust, love, and self-offering. Because this exploration takes place in the midst of a small group, you can expect increasingly to realize the blessings of mutual support, encouragement, guidance, and accountability in Christian community. Your growth in faith and maturation in spirit will benefit your congregation as well.

About the Resource and Process

Like all *Companions* resources, *The Way of Prayer* has two primary components: individual reading and daily exercises throughout the week with this Participant's Book and a weekly two-hour meeting based on directions in the Leader's Guide.

Each weekly chapter in the Participant's Book introduces new material and provides five daily exercises to help you reflect on your life in light of the chapter content. After the Preparatory Meeting of your group, you will begin a weekly cycle as follows: On day 1 you will be asked to read the article; on days 2–6 you will complete each of the five daily exercises (found at the end of each week's reading); on day 7 you will meet with your group.

The daily exercises aim to help you move from information (knowledge about) to experience (knowledge of). The time commitment for one daily exercise is approximately thirty minutes. An important part of this process involves keeping a personal notebook or journal in which you record reflections, prayers, and questions for later review and for reference at the weekly group meeting.

Weekly meetings include time for sharing reflections on the exercises of the past week and for moving deeper into the content of the article through various learning and prayer experiences. Meetings begin and end with simple worship times. You will need to bring your Participant's Book, your Bible, and your personal notebook or journal to each weekly group meeting. A resource list on pages 137–40 describes additional book titles related to the weekly themes.

The Companions in Christ Network

Another dimension of resources in the Companions series is the Network. The Network provides opportunities for you to share conversation and information. The Companions Web site, www.companionsinchrist.org, includes a discussion room where you can offer insights, voice questions, and respond to others in an ongoing process of shared learning. The site provides a list of other *Companions* groups journeying through each of the resources in the series and their geographical locations so that you can make connections as you feel led. Connecting in these ways will enrich your group's experience and the experience of those to whom you reach out. It will help you become aware of the wider reality of our companionship in the body of Christ across geographic and denominational lines.

Your Personal Notebook or Journal

Keeping a journal or notebook (commonly called journaling) will be one of the most important dimensions of your personal experience with

The Way of Prayer. The Participant's Book gives you daily spiritual exercises each week. More often than not, you will be asked to note your thoughts, reflections, questions, feelings, or prayers in relation to the exercise. Upper Room Books has made available a *Journal* that you may purchase. You will want, at minimum, something more permanent than a ring binder or paper pad.

You may find that this kind of personal writing quickly becomes second nature. Your thoughts may start to pour out of you, giving expression to an inner life that has never been released. If, on the other hand, you find the writing difficult or cumbersome, give yourself permission to try it in a new way. A journal is for your eyes only, so you may choose any style that suits you. You need not worry about beautiful words, good grammar, spelling, or even complete sentences. Jotting down key ideas, insights, or musings in a few words or phrases works just fine. You might doodle while you think or sketch an image that comes to you. Make journaling fun and relaxed! Remember, you have complete freedom to share with the group only what you choose of your reflections.

Keeping a journal as you move through *The Way of Prayer* is important for two reasons. First, the process of writing down thoughts clarifies them for us. Sometimes we really do not know what we think until we see our thoughts on paper, and often the process of writing generates new insight. Second, this personal record captures our inward experience over time so we can track changes in our thinking and growth. Memories are notoriously fragile and fleeting; specific feelings or creative connections we had two weeks ago or even three days ago can be hard to recall without a written record. Though your journal cannot capture all that goes through your mind in a single reflection period, it will offer reminders you can draw on during small-group meetings each week.

When you begin a daily exercise, have your journal and pen at hand. You need not wait until you have finished thinking an exercise through. Learn to stop and write as you go. Think on paper. Feel free to write anything that comes to you. Even ideas that seem off the topic may turn out to be more relevant than you first believed. If the process seems clumsy at first, keep an open mind. Like any spiritual practice, it grows easier over time; and its value becomes more apparent.

Your weekly practice of journaling is shaped as follows. On the first day after your group meeting, read the next week's article. Jot down your responses: "aha" moments, questions, points of disagreement, images, or any other reflections you wish to record. You may prefer to note these in the margins of the Participant's Book. Over the next five days, you will do the exercises for the week, recording responses as they are invited. On the day of the group meeting, it will help to review what you have written through the week, perhaps marking portions you would like to share in the group. Bring your journal with you to meetings so you can refer to it directly or refresh your memory about thoughts you want to paraphrase during discussion times. With time, you may find that journaling helps you discern more clearly your own pattern of living and how God is at work in your life.

Your Group Meeting

The weekly meeting is divided into four segments. First you will gather for a brief time of worship and prayer, which allows you to set aside the concerns of the day and center on God's guiding presence as you begin the group session.

The second segment of the meeting is called "Sharing Insights." During this time the group leader will invite you to talk about your experiences with the daily exercises. The leader will participate as a member and share his or her responses as well. Generally each member will briefly share thoughts and insights related to specific exercises. This process helps participants learn and practice what it means to listen deeply. You are a community of persons seeking to listen to God and to one another so that you can live more faithfully as disciples of Christ. The group provides a supportive community to explore your listening, your spiritual practices, and your efforts to employ those practices in daily life.

This community does not function as a traditional support group where people are sometimes quick to offer advice or to comment on one another's experiences. In *Companions* groups, members try to honor others' experiences through prayerful attentiveness, affirmation, and respectful clarifying questions. The "Sharing Insights" part of the meeting is less meaningful when persons interrupt and comment on what is being said or try to "fix" what they see as a problem (called "cross talk"). Group members are invited to trust the Holy Spirit's guidance and help one another listen to that guidance.

The "Sharing Insights" time presents a unique opportunity to learn how God works differently in each life. Our journeys, while varied, enrich others' experiences. Other people's faith stories allow us to see anew how God's activity touches or addresses our lives in unexpected ways. The group will establish some ground rules to facilitate this sharing. Participants need clearly to agree that each person will speak only about his or her own beliefs, feelings, and responses and that all group members have permission to share only what they choose and when they are ready to share. Above all, the group should maintain confidentiality so that what is shared stays in the group. Spouses or close friends in the same group will need to agree between themselves on permissible boundaries of confidentiality so that the choice to reveal oneself does not inadvertently reveal intimacies to the group without the other's consent.

The leader participates in this sharing and aids the process by listening and summarizing key insights that have surfaced. The leader closes this part of the meeting by calling attention to any patterns or themes that seem to have emerged from the group sharing. These patterns may point to a word God is offering the group.

The third segment of the meeting is called "Deeper Explorations." This part of the meeting gives group members an opportunity to explore a deeper dimension of God's grace, to practice related spiritual disciplines, or to explore implications of the week's theme for their church.

As it began, the group meeting ends with a brief time of worship. In this fourth segment members may lift to God the needs and concerns that emerge from the experience of the meeting itself or express the spiritual learning of the week through symbol, ritual, and prayer.

Invitation to the Journey

The weeks you give to *The Way of Prayer* will take you on a journey of genuine discovery: discovering dimensions of God's grace and presence you may not have previously known; discovering hidden aspects of your own heart and unearthing fresh insights; discovering common ground with your companions on this journey and learning more fully to respect the mystery of other persons in their unique differences. You will encourage one another to explore the depths of relationship with God and one another in prayer—a most precious privilege of faith. Naturally, the more you give to this process the more you will receive from it.

We cannot make such a journey fruitfully without the guidance of the risen Christ who walks continually beside us as we seek him. Nor can we benefit from this journey without the sustaining grace of the Holy Spirit who opens our ears and eyes to the deep truths of God. Our spiritual growth comes as we are gradually shaped more and more according to the image of Christ, the true and clear image of God (Col. 1:15). One of the great works of the Holy Spirit is to conform us to Christ (2 Cor. 3:18).

Therefore, we invite you to seek the grace of the Spirit as you begin *The Way of Prayer*. Open yourself inwardly to all God desires to give you as you explore the gift of prayer. Claim boldly what you believe you need in order to discover what God has in store for you and your companions in the weeks to come. And may grace abound for you!

Week 1

How Do You Pray?

My friend sat in the living room of her small apartment, gazing out the window at the ocean. Wrapped in an old homemade quilt, she held a cup of hot tea in her hands. Everything was silent except for the cry of the gulls. She has discovered she can sit for long periods of time, allowing the wonder of creation to fill her with gratitude. She told me later that she had no words for the experience but knew without a doubt that she was in the presence of God. "I've never before known the peace I felt on those mornings," she told me. "I think I was praying, but I've never heard prayer described that way. Could prayer be that simple and natural?"

Prayer is for nonexperts. It is possible . . . for the person with the slightest stirring of spiritual interest to begin to pray.
—Timothy Jones

Sometimes our experiences of God do not match the ideas of prayer we hold in our minds and hearts. What images do you have of people praying? Do you see them in Sunday worship with heads bowed as someone in front of the sanctuary offers the prayer? Do you imagine a person alone in her room sitting quietly before a candle? What about a group of young people singing their hearts out in a gospel choir? Or an elderly man lovingly holding his first great-grandchild? Have you ever seen a woman reading her Bible on the bus or a young child twirling on the grass, arms stretched high, shrieking with delight? Are all these people praying? What do you think?

Many of us understand and imagine prayer in fairly formal ways. We look to the Bible and to our Christian tradition to help us understand prayer. We read of Jesus teaching his disciples what we now know as the

Lord's Prayer. We think of our liturgical prayers: the call to worship, the pastoral prayers, the Great Thanksgiving, the benediction.

In addition to these prayers, you may remember a table grace or bedtime prayers you were taught as a child or instructions you received about how to pray. Someone might have told you that prayer is simply talking to God as a friend, and you discovered you could offer informal prayers out loud or in the quiet of your own heart.

Whatever your experiences of prayer, they will be the foundation from which to enter into this exploration of the way of prayer. I hope you will honor the ways you were taught to pray and celebrate the prayers of your tradition, that you will grow in your appreciation of both formal and informal prayers, and that you will expand your understanding of prayer to include many new ways to pray. I hope that you will come to recognize how each day presents many opportunities for prayer.

If you want a life of prayer, the way to get it is by praying. . . . You start where you are and you deepen what you already have.
—Thomas Merton

You might receive good news and utter a prayer of thanksgiving or hear bad news and cry out in despair. When facing a new challenge you might ask God for courage and strength; or, if a loved one is ill, plead for her health and wholeness. One day you might sigh in wonder at a flash of beauty and some other day raise your fist in anger when you witness the oppression of another. All these responses to the events of our lives are natural forms of prayer drawn from our hearts by a loving God who has been with us from the beginning of time.

Born Praying

The author of Psalm 139 proclaims God to be inescapable, ever present, and wise about our ways. God has searched us and knows us intimately, aware of all our thoughts, words, and actions. The psalmist writes, "It was you who formed my inward parts; you knit me together in my mother's womb" (Ps. 139:13). The author of the book of Acts agrees with the Hebrew scriptures and writes that God is not far from us, for "in him we live and move and have our being" (Acts 17:28).

Yet, if God is so present and so knowing, why do we pray at all? Doesn't God already know what we are thinking, feeling, and hoping for? One answer to this common question is that prayer is simply native to the human soul. Perhaps prayer is our natural human response to the gift of creation, beginning even before we become conscious. Ann and Barry Ulanov, authors of the book *Primary Speech,* believe that we are born into the world praying. They contend that as babies, our early coos, screams, and gurgles are our first prayers; they name these sounds "primary speech."

> Prayer is . . . primary in the sense that its speech includes . . . [an] unconscious voice that exists in us from the very beginning, from the moment of birth. This primary speech does not begin with words, but starts much earlier in human life, with instincts and emotions.[1]

If this is true, prayer in later years really involves remembering how to pray and expanding our prayer repertoire, rather than learning something entirely new. We will all grow beyond those early nonverbal sounds and think through our own reasons for prayer, but somewhere deep inside us resides the experience of being so deeply connected to God that we long to express the wonder of that relationship.

Across cultures and time people have found ways to express the joys and perplexities of their relationship with God. In the Judeo-Christian tradition we call those many ways of expressing this relationship with God *prayer*. Therefore we pray not because we believe it "works" or because we fear punishment if we don't pray or even because God commands it. We pray because we can. We pray because we must. As writer and philosopher Sam Keen wrote, "I don't *believe* in prayer. I only *do* it."[2]

We are all pray-ers and have been praying longer and in more ways than most of us realize. Since we are born into relationship with God, prayer is knit into the fiber of our being; and we have the opportunity to pray in an infinite number of ways. Some prayers will arise spontaneously; some will be learned from the teachings of parents and church leaders; and others will be stumbled upon as we move through life. We can also seek out new ways to pray by studying, discussing, and practicing prayer together in this *Companions in Christ* group. We will begin our explorations in prayer by reflecting on how we might honor, deepen, and strengthen our relationship with God.

Our relationships with others flow directly from our primal way of being, which for the Christian is prayer.
—W. Paul Jones

Prayer as Relationship

All prayer, formal and informal, is about our relationship with God. Thinking about building a relationship with another person may offer some clues about the ways we can deepen our relationship with God. One of the most common ways we participate in relationship is through honest and open verbal communication. When we want to draw close to someone, we tell that person about every aspect of our lives. In the beginning of a relationship we may share slowly to see if the other is trustworthy. We often hold back those things we fear will not be accepted. But over time, as we feel safer, we share more and more of who we are. As we become more honest, we recognize the wonder of being in relationship with one who accepts us and loves us unconditionally.

If you have ever had the painful experience of sharing something with another person that made you vulnerable, only to be dismissed, ridiculed, or rejected, you might have trouble trusting God with your inmost heart. Once I took the risk of telling a close friend how angry and hurt I felt as a result of the way she had treated me. She grew defensive, turned on me in anger, and soon after ended the friendship. It took me a long time to begin to trust other friends again, and for a while that experience made me wonder if I could trust God. Was it possible that the Holy One would respond to my feelings as my friend did, turning away in anger and ending our relationship? I had to risk speaking my whole truth to God to discover for myself that God was trustworthy. As I did that, I grew in trust; now I know that the divine presence is always willing to listen to and accept me as I am.

Experiences of becoming emotionally intimate with another person can guide us as we engage in our conversations with God. I believe the great Listener wants to hear all of our thoughts, feelings, and creative ideas. God can handle our anger and jealousy, our tears and our laughter, and wants us to speak about our shame and doubts as well as our love and gratitude. When we speak our truth to a loving presence, healing and growth can take place.

Becoming Silent

Greater comfort and ease in a relationship leads us to realize that we are called upon to listen as well as speak. We begin to put the needs of the other before our own, opening our hearts to listen as deeply as possible. In offering the gift of listening with the heart we may be surprised at what we receive from the other, such as hearing an idea or a story that challenges, affirms, or comforts us. In an intimate relationship, giving and receiving merge as both partners become willing to speak and to listen.

Listening calls us to silence, and sometimes in a close relationship both parties are silent at the same time. Think of a time when you fell into silence with another person—not the awkward silence of not knowing what to say or searching for words to express yourself but the comfortable silence that occurs when trust is deep and you need only the presence of the other. At such times speech is unnecessary, and the silence, rather than driving a wedge between two persons, binds them more closely together.

Silence can also build a relationship when we join with another in an activity that does not call for conversation. We grow closer when we garden side by side, each bent into a different chore, creating order and beauty together. Intimacy grows when we join our voices in song or when we link arms for support and walk silently through the snow. One of the warmest memories of my childhood is of my father and me reading together in the living room. We were not reading to each other or even reading the same thing. We were simply together, pursuing our own interests in the company of the other. Those evenings together deepened our relationship.

What we know about the gift of silence in strengthening our human relationships can help us recognize the value of silent prayer. We do not move into silence with God only for the purpose of listening to the Holy One but also to recognize the gift of God's being silently present with us. When we fall quiet in prayer, we usually want and expect to hear something. If God is silent we may believe we are doing something wrong. Maybe we aren't listening hard enough or in the right way. Are we hearing nothing because the Holy one has decided not to answer or doesn't like our question or request? Maybe the silence means God has abandoned us! Our inner voices search for reasons to explain the lack of divine response. I have come to believe that when we fall silent in prayer, God falls silent with us. Not in the awkward way of not knowing what to say, or the judgmental way of withholding words to punish. Rather, God is silent with us in trust and in love, knowing that what we need more than affirmation or advice is simply the divine presence. In silence, God gives us exactly that.

When we go to sit in silence, . . . we begin the process of allowing God to be the center of our world.
—Daniel Wolpert

We also strengthen our human relationships when we take on tasks or projects together. In working toward a common goal, people share an experience that brings them closer together. As my mother was dying, my sister and I joined our energy to get her the best care she could have and to make the life-and-death decisions she was unable to make for herself. After her death we took care of issues regarding her will, planned her memorial service, and told stories while laughing and crying together. During that time our hearts and minds were as one although we brought different gifts and skills to the tasks before us. We now see that experience as pivotal in forming the deep relationship we have today.

Think of some activities you have participated in that have drawn you more deeply into relationship. Perhaps building something together, planning celebrations, or working for change in the neighborhood helped you grow closer to others. Maybe you have found that travel provides the opportunity for intimacy or that dancing together creates a bond. A friend of mine told me about spending time with her two young grandchildren. The girls did not want her to play with them; they simply wanted her to watch them. "Grandma, Grandma! Watch me! Watch me! See what I can do!" The little ones valued her presence as a witness to their lives. My friend's ability to turn her loving attention on them strengthened their bond.

What can we learn from our life experience that will guide us in our relationship with God? How do these human activities translate into prayer? When we use our gifts and skills in the service of God with a lively sense of divine presence, we are praying. When we join with God and others to create beauty, promote peace, and act for justice, we are praying. We pray when we intentionally journey or "dance" with God, learning new steps and discovering the willingness to follow. We pray when we gratefully witness life unfolding within the wonder of creation. These activities draw us closer to God, for we have answered the call to align our minds and hearts as well as our hands, feet, and voices with God's promises for creation.

Prayer is not primarily saying words or thinking thoughts. It is, rather, a stance. It's a way of living in the Presence.
—Richard Rohr

Called into Prayer

All prayer begins with God. The Creator does not wait passively for us to come with our prayers; rather, our prayers are a response to God's call to us. God was with us in infancy, calling forth our response to divine love. After a few months we turned outward to our primary caregivers, responding to their love. As we grew older, we learned to attend to those who entered our lives and then began to forge a relationship with the wider world. Our growth outward was necessary for the full development of our humanity; but God has not let us forget our prerational experience of relationship and continually invites us back. Somewhere deep inside we long to return to our early intimacy with God.

Many years ago I heard the story of a four-year-old child who asked her parents if she could have some time alone with her new baby brother. They were hesitant but allowed her to go into the nursery and close the door. They turned on the intercom that connected the infant's room with theirs. They heard their daughter draw close to the crib. After a moment of silence she said to the new baby, "I need you to tell me about God. I'm starting to forget."

"As a deer longs for flowing streams, so my soul longs for you, O God" (Ps. 42:1), writes the psalmist. This longing of the human soul is our response to God's love and desire for us. This holy love activates our longing for God. Therefore, when people tell me they are not praying but long to pray, I tell them that their longing itself is a prayer. Their hearts have responded to God's call into relationship. Understanding where prayer begins makes praying easier and more natural. Instead of figuring out how to invite God to be with us, we have only to say yes to the divine invitation.

Often prayer begins as a longing in the heart, a longing for love, . . . a longing to make contact with a Power greater than ourselves.
—Mark Yaconelli and Alexx Campbell

Scripture can help us see the power and grace of this invitation. Recall the response of Simon and his brother, Andrew, both fishermen, to Jesus' call to relationship. The Gospel of Mark tells us that "immediately they left their nets and followed him" (Mark 1:18). Jesus called, and they said yes. Once together they moved more deeply into relationship with words and silence, shared activities, misunderstandings, and growing faith. Their journey through hardship, disappointment, wonder, and delight deepened into intimacy. Such is our journey of prayer.

Just as the disciples were often confused by Jesus' teachings and unable to receive his love, we will at times distance ourselves from God. Other concerns may seem more important; we get caught up in the struggles, joys, and sheer busyness of life. When we do not receive the desired response in prayer, we may intentionally turn away from God in frustration or anger. Sometimes we simply forget about God, living as if our activities were all-important. Yet, God keeps calling and actively searching for us just as the woman in the parable of the lost coin searches for what she has lost (Luke 15:8-10). When the woman loses one of her ten coins, she lights her lamp and carefully sweeps the house searching for the lost coin. When she finds it, she calls together her friends and neighbors saying, "Rejoice with me, for I have found the coin that I had lost" (v. 9).

God's love and desire for us is never ending. God calls us into relationship right now. We do not need to get dressed up, clean the house, or make any other preparations. All we have to do is accept the gracious invitation to come as we are. Whenever and in whatever way we say yes, we are in prayer.

Pray as you can,
not as you can't.
—Dom John Chapman

I have been drawing on our experience of human relationships to help us understand the many ways we relate to God in prayer. However, we must always be aware that God is much more than even the most wonderful friend we can imagine. God is not only the "Other" with whom we can build an intimate relationship; God is also within us, as close as our breath and as integral as the beating of our hearts. The analogy of prayer to human relationship helps us begin a discussion of the way of prayer, but it does not do full justice to the wonder and mystery of our sacred Source. Next week we will explore in depth other images of God to help us understand our need for a variety of ways to pray.

DAILY EXERCISES

This week's article and exercises encourage you to recall and explore your experience of prayer, along with your ways of thinking about what prayer is or is not. Read Week 1, "How do You Pray?" before you begin these reflection exercises in the days that follow. Use your journal to record thoughts and questions as you read the week's assignment and then to respond to each daily exercise. Enter these practices in a spirit open to the real presence of God, the risen Christ, and the living Spirit.

Exercise 1 People Pray

Read and review different experiences of prayer in the Bible (see Genesis 18:16-33; 32:22-32; 1 Samuel 1:9-18; Psalms 19; 22; 23; Isaiah 6:1-8; Matthew 4:1-11; 6:5-14; Mark 14:32-42; Luke 18:9-14). In your journal name the prayer experiences in the Bible that you find most meaningful personally.

Reflect on your own experiences of prayer and where they connect with what you found in the Bible. Reflect in your journal on points of connection.

In a few moments of quiet prayer remember and imagine that God is reaching out to connect with you. Recall with thanksgiving the times you've been most aware of the God connection and what conditions or practices, if any, facilitated the encounter. Record your thoughts.

Exercise 2 Nature Prays

Read Psalm 148. This psalm invites all creation to praise God. Similarly, the text of the hymn "All Creatures of Our God and King," a beautiful prayer by Saint Francis of Assisi, celebrates how all elements of nature have the capacity to praise, each by doing what comes naturally.[3]

Imagine how various plants and animals assume postures of prayer: trees swaying in the breeze, flowers turning faces toward the sun, birds perching on telephone wires, puppies curling up in warm places. Feel free to look out the window or to find a place outdoors for inspiration. You may want to describe or draw some examples in your journal.

Experiment with a prayer position that you see in nature. For instance, stand and sway; sit and look upward; curl yourself into a tight little ball. See how this new, natural posture guides your prayer. Spend several minutes offering your thoughts and feelings to God. Be aware of the Creator's presence and record any insights in your journal.

Exercise 3 Actions Pray

Read Micah 6:8. Micah instructs us "to do justice, and to love kindness, and to walk humbly with [our] God." To "walk humbly with . . . God" may mean to carry out daily activities as though we were doing them hand in hand with God, seeking to walk in the world as God would walk.

Think back over the activities of the past week. Where were you most aware and least aware of God in the midst of your busyness? When did you have a sense of acting in concert with God's spirit? Jot down your memories in your journal.

Take a moment to ask God what activity you and God could share today. Sit quietly and listen. Write down and take seriously what comes to mind, whether playful, unusual, or challenging. Be sure to carve out space in your day for participating in that activity with a sense of walking humbly with God.

Exercise 4 Silence Speaks

Read Matthew 6:6. In this verse Jesus instructs his disciples to "go into your room and shut the door." Additionally, Psalm 46:10 proclaims, "Be still, and know that I am God!" Elijah encounters God in unexpected, profound silence (1 Kings 19:11-13). Jesus frequently goes off by himself to pray (Luke 5:16).

Do as Jesus says in Matthew 6:6. Find a quiet place where you will be undisturbed (if only for a few minutes). Choose a comfortable prayer position. For ten minutes be silent before God in all honesty, allowing God to see who you really are. When distractions enter your mind, repeat the phrase *Be still* to quiet your soul.

When your time of stillness feels complete, spend some time journaling. Describe your experience of silence. Was it peaceful? difficult? comforting? frustrating? refreshing? In what ways does silence make you more aware of what is going on inside you? In what ways does silence make you more aware of God?

Exercise 5 Prayer Risks

The author of Psalm 139 reminds us that God's presence is inescapable, that God knows even the most private things about us yet loves us anyway.

Choose a prayer space and a prayer posture that will allow you to be truly yourself in the presence of God. Read Psalm 139 and meditate for a few moments on any verse that touches you. Risk approaching God prayerfully in trust and love to share one thing with God that you have never shared before. Spend some silent time listening in God's presence and knowing that you are loved for all that you are. If you don't feel ready to risk sharing a deep secret, then spend a few minutes talking with God about fears or obstacles that you face. How can God help you draw closer? Write your reflections in your journal.

Remember to review your journal entries for the week in preparation for the group meeting.

Week 2
Images of God

The universe reflects the wonder and the mystery of God—in the stars above, the earth on which we live, the beauty and complexity of creatures large and small, and the amazing diversity in humanity. Look upward on a clear and moonless night. Press your nose against a glass tank holding myriad species of fish. Notice the size and the stillness of trees. Smile at the people you pass on the street. To live in creation with our senses awake and aware is to know the wondrous presence of God.

Prayer is the context in which we ask God again and again the question John's disciples posed to Jesus: "Where do you dwell?"
—John S. Mogabgab

As awesome and powerful as the Creator is, we also know God to be loving, compassionate, and forgiving. We learn of these qualities of God through Gospel stories, the wisdom of the Christian tradition, and our own living. Maybe you have experienced the grace of forgiveness after making a bad mistake. Likely you have known God's love through the kindness of friends or strangers. When grieving, perhaps you have felt the compassion of God's embrace that helps you know that your tears have healing power.

These images of God invite us into an intimate relation with the Holy One. But for some people these images have been distorted and narrowed by the teachings of others. "I want to believe God loves me and is calling me into a loving relationship," a young woman told me on retreat. "But that is not the image of God I grew up with. The God of my childhood was a judge and scorekeeper, watching and making note of all I did wrong. I was terrified of God, and I prayed to appease God—not to grow closer." She went on to tell the group that although she had been told of God's love, the old images had not completely disappeared. They made her wonder if she wanted to pray in ways that could deepen her relationship with God. "What if I make myself vulnerable and God turns out to be critical and punishing?" she asked. "I get pulled between desire and fear and am not sure where to turn." Sorting out for ourselves who we believe God to be is an important part of the exploration of prayer.

Trusting the Scriptural Witness to Christ

As Christians we turn to Christ to help us know God more fully, for as Paul wrote, "[Christ] is the image of the invisible God, the firstborn of all creation" (Col. 1:15). Jesus' life and ministry illuminate the mercy and compassion of God. Jesus saw the pain and sorrow of people of all walks of life and reached out to heal those struggling with life's burdens. In the Gospel of Luke we read of Jesus laying his hands upon a woman who had been bent over for eighteen years and saying to her, "Woman, you are set free from your ailment" (Luke 13:12). Jesus broke the conventions of his day by touching and talking with women, visiting and eating with outcasts (Matt. 26:6), and befriending tax collectors (Matt. 11:19). He interacted with sinners, offering them forgiveness and new life. When the religious leaders threatened the woman caught in adultery, Jesus admonished them to become aware of their own sins by examining their hearts and lives. The men turned away, leaving her alone with Jesus who said to her, "Neither do I condemn you. Go your way, and from now on do not sin again" (John 8:11).

Jesus' refusal to enact retribution against his enemies revealed God's radical compassion. He told his disciples, "You have heard that it was said, 'You shall love your neighbor and hate your enemy.' But I say to you, Love your enemies and pray for those who persecute you, so that you may be children of your Father in heaven; for he makes his sun rise on the evil and on the good, and sends rain on the righteous and on the unrighteous" (Matt. 5:43-45). Jesus Christ is the embodiment of God's love for all of us, at all times, in all situations.

God's love is the starting point and ending point of all prayer.
—Roberta C. Bondi

In addition to the living Christ revealing God's nature, we can learn from Jesus' intimate relationship with his Abba. Early in his life Jesus responded to God's call to relationship by remaining in the Temple after his parents have left. When they returned for him he said, "Why were you searching for me? Did you not know that I must be in my Father's house?" (Luke 2:49). Later in his life Jesus experienced the outpouring of God's love at the moment of his baptism in the Jordan River (Luke 3:21-22), and again in the desert before the beginning of his ministry (Luke 4:1-14).

Throughout his ministry Jesus relied on this loving relationship with God. He told his followers, "I can do nothing on my own. As I hear, I judge; and my judgment is just, because I seek to do not my own will but the will of him who sent me" (John 5:30). Jesus sought solace and strength from his Abba through prayer. He would leave his hectic life to spend time alone with God. "In the morning, while it was still very dark, he got up and went out to a deserted place, and there he prayed" (Mark 1:35).

By looking to the life and the teachings of Jesus and trusting the truth of the Gospels, we can heal negative pictures of God that might interfere with our developing intimacy with God through prayer. The witness of the Word made flesh opens us to new ways of thinking about the divine presence and helps us engage in different forms of prayer, discovering for ourselves what prayer reveals about the nature of God.

Trusting Your Experience in Prayer

Someone once said that the image we hold of God determines how we pray and what we pray for. For example, an image of a loving and forgiving God who longs to be in relationship with us invites us into prayer that nurtures intimacy. Trusting in God's acceptance and forgiveness frees us to offer prayers of confession. We can dance our prayers with the assurance that God invites and welcomes us as valued partners and sing praises knowing our Creator desires that all of creation experience wholeness and healing.

However, if I imagine God to be critical, watching for my mistakes and calling me into the divine presence only to be judged, I will try to hide my shortcomings and pray only those things I think God wants to hear. Fearing God's anger and punishment, I may attempt to offer prayers designed to please and placate. Other images of God can stunt our prayer life as well. If I think of the Creator as distant and impersonal, a deity who once set the universe in motion and now watches it unfold according to immutable laws, then I am unlikely to pray at all. If I think of God as

Prayer is drawing near to God; this cannot take place in the midst of fear.
—James Emery White

a giant wish-dispenser or heavenly Santa, I might use my prayers to try to get God to do what I want. None of these images creates intimacy. Rather, they promote dishonest, passive, and manipulative prayers, impeding the open communication, vulnerability, and trust that mark the healthy human-divine relationship we see in the Gospels.

As you are introduced to different forms of prayer in the weeks to come, pay attention to your feelings and intuitions and trust that your experiences in prayer will be guided by the Holy Spirit who prays in us according to God's will (Rom. 8:26-27). See if you can set aside preconceived ideas about God and let the prayer itself guide you into new understandings of the divine nature. Through your experience of prayer, your images of God may become more varied, allowing your prayer life to expand and deepen.

Expanding Images and Names of God

The book of Exodus records Moses' meeting with God on the mountain, and his request that the divine name be revealed. "God said to Moses, 'I AM WHO I AM'" (Exod. 3:14). This passage has guided me to imagine God as a multifaceted prism with an infinite number of faces, each side reflecting another image or name of the great I AM. No single name captures the fullness of God, but each image can guide our prayers.

The most basic question when it comes to prayer is to whom do we pray?
—James Emery White

For example, depending on my prayer needs I choose different names for God. When seeking forgiveness, I direct my prayers to Merciful One. Needing inspiration I simply say, "Come, Holy Spirit" and remain in silence. A friend of mine who lost her beloved brother to cancer found herself praying to Jesus, My Brother, as she sought courage and strength.

In addition to choosing a name for God to fit our prayers, we can address God in different ways and see what words might follow. I frequently invite this activity on prayer retreats, giving participants a variety of names for the Holy One and encouraging them to write a brief prayer after each image. People are often surprised by the prayers that are drawn from their hearts when they use different names for God. Listen to the simple and beautiful prayers that emerged from one group:

God of the Stillness: *Quiet my soul.*
Lord of the Dance: *Lead, and I will follow.*

Gentle Shepherd: *Watch over me.*
My Rock and My Salvation: *Teach me to cling to you.*
Compassionate Listener: *I trust you with my secrets.*
Weaver/Spinner God: *Unravel the tangles of my relationships and help me create new patterns of reconciliation.*
Blessed Healer: *I need balm for my soul.*
Inner Light: *Burn bright in me and let me shine.*

All of these prayers imagine God as "holy other," someone with whom we are in a sacred and life-giving relationship. In the activity above I invited the group to suggest names that touch hearts and invite intimacy. Images such as the Rock to Which We Cling or the Light Within bring God very close. They point to the immanence or nearness of God. But sometimes we want to acknowledge the transcendence of God, so we use images that honor the immense and infinite divine nature. We might use this language when we long to praise our Creator for the goodness of the earth or find new ways to see the world with holy compassion. Then we could address our prayers to Lord of the Universe, Great Visionary, or God of All the Nations. Such images help us know that God is far beyond all we can imagine even while present in ordinary life.

Immanence and Transcendence

Perceiving God as both present with us and far beyond us may seem a contradiction, but it is really a paradox—two seeming opposites held together in a larger truth. We can explore this paradox more fully by pondering God's nature through the Bible, the tradition of church writings, our own God-given reason, and our experience.

The first chapter of the Bible starts, "In the beginning when God created the heavens and the earth . . . " (Gen. 1:1). This passage clearly indicates a transcendent God existing beyond all of creation, separating light from darkness, sky from earth, and water from land. Yet only a few chapters later we find an immanent God "walking in the garden at the time of the evening breeze," calling out to Adam and Eve with intimate nearness (Gen. 3:8-9).

Another of my favorite scripture texts is the story of Jesus' baptism, where in one passage we are given both a transcendent and immanent image of God: "And when Jesus had been baptized, just as he came up from the water, suddenly the heavens were opened to him and he saw the Spirit of God descending like a dove and alighting on him. And a voice from heaven said, 'This is my Son, the Beloved, with whom I am well pleased'" (Matt. 3:16-17). At this moment God is in heaven speaking from afar, and at the same time right at the Jordan "alighting on him."

The paradox of God's transcendence and immanence is expressed simply in words penned by German theologian Dietrich Bonhoeffer from a Nazi prison cell, "God is [the] beyond in the midst of our life."[1] Words spoken twenty years later by Thomas Merton may help us penetrate Bonhoeffer's comment: "We are living in a world that is absolutely transparent, and God is shining through it all the time. . . . God shows Himself everywhere, in everything—in people and in things and in nature and in events."[2] Through the centuries theologians and spiritual writers have attempted to clarify the mystery of divine transcendence and immanence. Marcus Borg, a contemporary scholar, comments, "God is not to be identified with the sum total of things. Rather, God is more than everything, even as God is present everywhere. God is all around us and within us, and we are within God."[3]

The adoration of God in prayer is a mixture of gratitude and reverence and awe.
—Douglas V. Steere

Looking to your own reason and experience of God, I imagine you can identify both sides of the paradox. Personally, I love offering praise and worship to a wondrous and mysterious God far beyond my understanding. I find it comforting that this Transcendent One calls me into a loving relationship—beckoning, wooing, and pursuing me. At these times I experience God as beyond me. We are separate, not one. But other times I sense no distance or separation from God. I often feel God's immediate presence when I am in nature, opening all my senses to the beauty of creation. I have known God in the embrace of a loved one or the tender touch of a comforting friend. During Holy Communion I am filled with the wonder of God in the breaking of bread and am reminded of the words of the psalm that says, "Taste and see that the Lord is good" (Ps. 34:8). In kneeling to partake of the elements, I receive assurance of God's presence at the table through the sacrificial love of Christ; we become as one, no longer separate.

Jesus said, "Abide in me as I abide in you. Just as the branch cannot bear fruit by itself unless it abides in the vine, neither can you unless you abide in me" (John 15:4). Even in our most intimate spiritual union, the life and spirit of Christ transcend us. As we ponder the paradox of God's transcendence and immanence, I say simply that God is in you, yet you are not God. God is in all of creation, yet creation is not God; God is more than creation. Our theological affirmation of the transcendence and immanence of God deeply influences the way we pray. The nearness of God gives us courage to speak our hearts honestly and confidently, yet the transcendence of God keeps us from imagining that prayer is just a cozy two-way relationship. We need the balance and tension of this paradox to enter the lifelong adventure of praying to the living God.

A Theology of Prayer

We may think of theology as an abstract study of God that highly trained people do in academic settings. But we are thinking theologically this week in our exploration of the way of prayer. You will be asked to reflect on who God is in your life and to recognize the connection between your ideas about God, your experiences of God, and the ways you pray to God. As you seek to discover your own theology, allow yourself to be guided by the life of Jesus and his intimate relationship with his Abba whom he knew to be loving, compassionate, and forgiving. As you explore the many possible ways to pray, take comfort from Paul's assurance that when "we do not know how to pray as we ought . . . [the] Spirit intercedes with sighs too deep for words" (Rom. 8:26).

Our theological reflection will use heart as well as head, intuition as well as volition as we seek to know our Maker. But remember that in spite of all the ways we try to understand God, the Holy One will remain a mystery. Theologian and author Marjorie Suchocki asks that we be satisfied with "sufficient knowledge," suggesting that "the partial and relative nature of our knowledge does not invalidate our knowing."[4] If we act on the knowledge we have, we can trust the Spirit to deepen and strengthen our relationship with God in prayer.

During these weeks, continue to reflect theologically on your experiences of prayer. With each new method of prayer ask yourself how its practice reveals another aspect of the nature of God or the heart of Christ. Play with the images; hold them lightly; allow them to shift and change. Notice old images that restrict your prayer experience, and pay attention to any spontaneous stretching or healing of your God-images.

We all come to prayer with different experiences of and names for God. We all come in need of some kind of healing or expansion of our images. In our explorations we will not all arrive at the same theological conclusions. But within the differences, I pray that at the core of your own unique theology of prayer you will know a God of love. After years of study, exploration, and healing, Roberta Bondi came to this conclusion about the nature of God:

> Before anything else, above all else, beyond everything else, God loves us. God loves us extravagantly, ridiculously, without limit or condition. . . . God does not love us "in spite of who we are" or "for whom God knows we can become." . . . God loves us, the very people we are; and not only that, but, even against what we ourselves sometimes find plausible, God likes us.[5]

This doesn't mean God likes everything we do or that God does not exercise judgment in love. It does mean God desires above all to be in a deep, abiding, growing relationship of love with us. Prayer is the expression of this relationship. We have been created for such communion.

The result of prayer is to discover reasons for loving God.
—Isaac of Syria

DAILY EXERCISES

This week's reading and exercises invite you to think broadly about how you perceive and relate to God, how your images of God impact your prayer, and what it might mean to expand your ways of naming God. Read Week 2, "Images of God," before you begin these reflection exercises in the days that follow. Record in your journal the thoughts, feelings, and questions that arise as you read the article and complete the daily exercises. Begin each exercise by taking a moment to center yourself in God's presence.

Exercise 1 God Is Far and Near

Read Genesis 1:1–2:4 and Genesis 2:4-25. The opening chapters of Genesis vividly portray God's transcendence and immanence. The first account shows us a God who creates by simply speaking the words *Let there be light.* The second reveals a God who physically touches and breathes life into creation.

Skim the first account (Gen. 1:1–2:4) and look for glimpses of God's character. In your journal, make a list of adjectives that describe God in this reading. Then skim the second account (Gen. 2:4-25) and write a second list. Compare the two descriptions of God; ponder the paradox of transcendence and immanence. Record your thoughts.

Close with a prayer that acknowledges the mystery of who God is.

Exercise 2 God Has Many Names

Read Psalm 145:1-3. "Every day I will bless you," sings the psalmist, "and praise your name forever and ever." The Bible offers us many names for God (see Exodus 3:14; 33:17-23; Psalm 144:1-2; Isaiah 9:6; 45:15; Matthew 1:23; Luke 2:21; John 14:16-17). List in your journal as many names for God as you can find in the Bible and in hymns as well.

Review the names you have found and prayerfully say them aloud as acts of adoration. Which names seem to draw you closer to God? Which ones push you away? In your journal capture your thoughts and feelings about each name.

Complete the exercise by sitting prayerfully before God, whose mystery transcends all names we would give.

Exercise 3 God Appears

Read Colossians 1:15-20. Closely related to names for God are the divine images we hold in our minds and hearts. Review some of the Bible's rich ways of imagining God and list as many as you can find. (See Genesis 2:4-9; 19:13; Exodus 3:1-6; 13:21-22; Psalms 23; 131; Song of Solomon 2:16-17; Isaiah 6:1-3; 49:15-16; Jonah 1; Matthew 5:48; Mark 1:11; Luke 15:20-24; John 4:13-15; Col. 1:15-20; 1 John 1:5; 4:7-12.)

Identify the images you respond to most forcefully either positively or negatively, and note in your journal the reasons for the strong feelings. Choose your favorite image of God from any source and draw a picture of it. Then take a few moments to practice being aware of God's presence.

Exercise 4 God Reveals

Read Luke 18. With nearly every action and teaching, Jesus challenged divine images that failed God and harmed people. In this scripture passage, which images of God does Jesus challenge and what fresh images of God does Jesus present? Capture your insights in your journal.

Which images of God do you resist? Let your journal be a place where you examine your responses. Close your eyes and imagine yourself in the presence of Jesus, who wants to open the way for your relationship with God. Offer Jesus the images you resist, and share how they affect you. Pay attention to what Jesus says to you, shows you, or gives you in exchange.

Exercise 5 Prayer Stretches

Read Genesis 32:22-32. Enter imaginatively into this passage where God asks Jacob's name and Jacob asks God the same. Imagine God's asking you, "What is your name?" Sit with the question for a while. Reflect in your journal on how you would name your real self before God.

Then imagine yourself asking God in turn, "What is your name?" Be silent before the mystery of God; wait and listen. If it would help, look back over the names and images from this week's exercises. Write what your heart is telling you.

Review your journal entries for the week for the group meeting.

Week 3

Praying by Heart

I was in my early forties when my heart began doing strange things. For no apparent reason it would begin to beat in double time. The first time it happened, I felt that surely I was dying. My heart beat faster and faster until I thought it would explode. Then suddenly it returned to its normal rate, leaving me shaken and afraid. Later I was diagnosed with tachycardia, a non-life-threatening condition that I would simply learn to live with. So I did, but how much more attention I began to pay to the beating of my heart!

For many years the episodes of rapid heartbeat happened infrequently. Then in my fifties they began to occur more often, increasing finally to two or three times a week. I began to live with my fingers poised above my pulse wondering when my heart would make itself known again. I constantly attended to the beating of my heart. By my early sixties the episodes had increased to the point that my cardiologist recommended a procedure to cure the tachycardia. Now, thanks to modern medicine, I am free from those frightening episodes. However, I continue to pay attention to my heart—only now I do it in gratitude not fear.

When our hearts beat constantly and consistently, we tend to forget the miracle of the life force within us. We take the steady beating for granted, rarely even thinking about it. And yet when we pay attention, our hearts can teach us about the wonder of God, as the following hymn verse written by Thomas H. Troeger proclaims:

> Through our beating hearts remind us
> that the source of all our powers
> is, O God, your vital Spirit
> that is animating ours.

Every pulse beat is revealing
while we work and while we rest
that your care for us is constant
and to live is to be blest.[1]

The heart is both physical reality *and* metaphor for the center of our inner life. To move from head to heart is to move from the conscious rational intellect to the core where feeling, thought, intuition, and intention all unite.

When we pray by heart, our attention on God moves from the mind to the heart, allowing our hearts to pray for us. We are no longer in charge. Rather, we give ourselves over to the Holy Spirit and experience the wisdom Paul refers to in his letter to the Roman Christians: "For we do not know how to pray as we ought, but that very Spirit intercedes with sighs too deep for words" (8:26). One of the earliest forms of prayer in Christianity facilitates this process of moving from head to heart. It is called the Jesus Prayer, or the Prayer of the Heart.

The Jesus Prayer . . . rises from the deepest place of our being . . . for that is what the heart *means, not our physical heart.*
—Irma Zaleski

The Jesus Prayer

The Jesus Prayer comes to us from the Eastern Orthodox church tradition. It is a brief prayer that combines praise, petition, and confession. The most common form is "Lord Jesus Christ, Son of God, have mercy on me, a sinner" or "Jesus, have mercy." This simple prayer finds its basis in scripture (Luke 18:13, 38) and "says all that needs to be said to promote mindfulness of who Jesus is, who the one praying is, and what the relationship between them is."[2] To practice the Jesus Prayer, simply pray it constantly as you go about your daily life—as you awaken, prepare your morning meal, go to work, do errands, take a walk, play with the children, visit with friends. The prayer accompanies you in all you do. Over time, through the ongoing repetition of the prayer, the words slowly sink from your head to your heart—moving from rational consciousness to the deep center of your being where it begins to pray itself.

The transforming process of praying in this way is delightfully described in *The Way of a Pilgrim*, a short narrative written by a nineteenth-century Russian peasant.[3] The peasant longs to learn what the apostle Paul meant when he advised us to pray without ceasing. He seeks help from the superior of a small monastery who teaches him the Jesus Prayer and tells him to repeat these words until the prayer moves from the mind to the heart. The pilgrim takes this advice seriously and wanders across Russia practicing the prayer. At times he tracks his repetitions of the prayer by using a circle of one hundred beads.

On his journey the pilgrim meets people who help him and people who hinder his progress. But through all his adventures he perseveres in the practice of the Jesus Prayer and eventually realizes that his heart is praying constantly. Overflowing with wonder and joy, the pilgrim continues his travels eager to share his experience with others so that they might also experience the glory of God's grace.[4]

Pray without ceasing *(1 Thess. 5:17, NRSV), enjoined the apostle. Take this seriously. Become prayer.*
—Wendy M. Wright

Personalizing the Prayer of the Heart

When I first encountered the Jesus Prayer and *The Way of a Pilgrim,* I was eager to try that method of praying without ceasing; but I found the wording of the prayer difficult to repeat. At that time I was recovering from a pervasive sense of shame and guilt, struggling to know myself as a beloved child of God. The words of the Jesus Prayer seemed to reinforce my old habitual feelings of unworthiness, and I found them hard to pray. A wise teacher suggested that I find words to fit my own experience of praise, petition, and confession and use those words instead.

I wrestled with this suggestion, wondering what right I had to change the words of an ancient prayer. I also wondered if not liking the words might actually be an excuse for not engaging in prayer of the heart. In spite of these reservations I believed that the practice of a heart prayer was what I needed at that difficult time. So, after much struggle, I discovered my own prayer. I chose to praise God with the title *Gracious.* I recognized my petition must be for healing. Then I confessed that I was God's beloved daughter. These thoughts seemed daring. Who was I to claim a loving relationship with God? But the thoughts felt right, and I began to pray, "Gracious God, heal me, your beloved daughter."

Over the years I have taught others about the Jesus Prayer, and many have found freedom in changing the words to fit their own experience. One person chose "Jesus, my brother, walk with me." Another wrote "Holy Spirit, fill me," and still another "Lord Jesus, open my closed heart."

After praying a prayer of the heart for a period of time, some pilgrims discover that the words they have chosen no longer fit their experience. Their lives and their needs have changed. This change occurred for me when I realized a few years ago that the traditional prayer no longer seemed foreign and did not threaten me. I had received God's gracious healing and could recognize my sinfulness and need for mercy. Now I am able to pray, "Lord Jesus Christ, have mercy on me, a sinner."

Regularity is more sustaining in prayer than intensity or length.
—Roberta C. Bondi

Inward repetition of the Jesus Prayer daily over a long period of time allows the prayer to descend into the heart. When this happens, the prayer simply begins to pray itself. Every heartbeat expresses the joy of our relationship with God. Prayer of the heart can also come as a gift of grace. Have you ever discovered a prayer emerging from your heart into your mind? Maybe as you walk down the street, a phrase from scripture arises from your heart. You might be in the midst of a difficult task and a hymn begins singing itself in your soul. For these spontaneous prayers of the heart, we can only give thanks. Quaker author Richard Foster describes this experience when he writes, "It is the Holy Spirit who creates this prayer, and it is the Holy Spirit who sustains it."[5]

Breath Prayer

The Russian peasant in *The Way of a Pilgrim* discovered that his breath supported his practice of the Jesus Prayer. He would connect the words to his breathing to form a rhythm as he walked: "Lord Jesus Christ" on the inhale, "Son of God" on the exhale, "have mercy on me" inhaled, and "a sinner" exhaled. This is why you will sometimes hear the Jesus Prayer referred to as a breath prayer as well as a prayer of the heart. Both names for repetitive prayers are accurate; just as our heartbeat reveals to us the source of our powers, so our breathing reminds us of the nearness of God.

As we sometimes take for granted the beating of our hearts, we also can take for granted our breathing. I remember thinking how silly my dance teacher was to say in the middle of our expressive movements, "Don't forget to breathe." But as she continued to call us to awareness of our breath, I realized the many ways I would hold my breath, breathe only into the top of my lungs, or breathe rapidly when I became anxious.

As I paid attention to my breathing and learned new ways to breathe, I discovered how my breath could support my movements, allowing more flexibility, strength, and endurance. And so it is with prayer. Our breathing supports our practice.

Breath prayers are a modern adaptation of the ancient prayer of the heart. We create them to express our deepest needs. They help us keep God in the foreground amidst our daily living and clarify our relationship with the holy. Most breath prayers are six to eight syllables and fit easily into one inhale and exhale. Some examples are "Help me rest; give me peace," "Make clear my way, O Holy One," "Out of darkness, into light," or "Fill me, Spirit, with your love."

Ron DelBene, who has written extensively on this prayer method, suggests the following steps in creating or discovering your personal breath prayer:[6]

(1) Sit comfortably, close your eyes, and remember that God loves you and you are in God's presence.

(2) Imagine God calling you by name, asking "(Your name), what do you want?"

(3) Answer God honestly with whatever word or phrase comes from deep within you.

(4) Choose your favorite or most natural name for God.

(5) Combine your name for God with your word or phrase to form a brief prayer that flows smoothly. Examples:

What I Want	Name for God	Possible Prayer
Peace	God	Let me know your peace, O God.
Love	Jesus	Jesus, let me feel your love.
Guidance	Eternal Light	Eternal Light, guide me in your way.

Repeat the prayer for a few minutes, allowing the words to settle into a regular rhythm.

If more than one idea arises, you may need to ponder what the *deepest* desire of your heart is. A helpful question to ask is, What do I want that will make me feel most whole? In creating your own breath prayer, you might take several days of reflection to discover what is best for you. Be patient, and let the words emerge from your deepest longings. When you have discovered your prayer, begin to practice it at different times during the day. You might pray it before you get out of bed in the morning. Or try turning off the car radio and pray while you drive. You could breathe and pray when you become anxious, frustrated, or bored. The breath prayer reminds us that praying is as natural as breathing.

Scripture Phrases

Short passages from the Bible offer rich material for breath prayers. Most of us have our favorite scriptures to which we can turn for a six-to-eight-syllable prayer. You may need to vary the words slightly to make the passage your own: "Come and find rest for your soul" (see Matt. 11:29), "You shall mount up with wings like eagles" (see Isa. 40:31), or "God plans for me a future with hope" (see Jer. 29:11).

The psalms are a rich resource for creating breath prayers and present us with the challenge of picking a phrase that holds special meaning. Sometimes you may have missed these phrases due to the length of the psalm. Psalm 27 is a wondrous prayer of celebration that ends with the words "Be strong, and let your heart take courage" (v. 14). In Psalm 42 we read the comforting words "My soul longs for you, O God" (v. 1). Either of these phrases could become a breath prayer.

Sometimes, instead of searching for a scripture passage to use as a breath prayer, you might allow a phrase to find you. Listen for words that especially touch your heart in Sunday worship and use them as your breath prayer for the week. When reading the Bible during a morning prayer time, let yourself discover a phrase you had not noticed before. Stay connected to the word of God by breathing that phrase as a prayer throughout your day's activities. A friend of mine who attends mass every morning listens for a phrase in the reading, turning it into her breath prayer for that day.

The presence of God is like the atmosphere we breathe.
—Thomas Keating

As you reflect on the various ways of praying with the heart and breath, you may be drawn to all of them. I can imagine your wanting to pray the Jesus Prayer in its traditional form or in words that express your own longings. A phrase for a breath prayer may have popped into your mind while reading this chapter, and maybe a favorite scripture passage as well. Then you might have thought of the wonderful possibility of having a new breath prayer every day or each week from your devotional time or Sunday worship. You cannot do them all. You will have to choose. To follow all these ideas would leave you scattered and frustrated, defeating the purpose of praying by heart: discovering your heart's deep prayer and allowing the Spirit to lead you to the joy of praying without ceasing.

There is a way of ordering our mental life on more than one level at once. On one level we may be meeting all the demands of external affairs. But deep within, . . . we may also be in prayer and adoration . . . and a gentle receptiveness to divine breathings.
—Thomas Kelly

Praying Always

Like the Russian peasant, modern Christians want to understand what the apostle Paul meant when he wrote that we are to pray without ceasing. Most of us will not leave the joys and responsibilities of our lives to wander the country praying the Jesus Prayer. We need to discover for ourselves how to integrate praying by heart into our lives.

We may be afraid that unceasing prayer will interfere with our daily tasks or that our activities will hinder prayer. We may wonder how our minds can focus on two things at once. Benedictine Sister Mary Margaret Funk tells us that "when the mind needs to be attentive to other work, the Jesus Prayer will drop down in consciousness and the brain will activate a clear mental process for the business at hand." Instead of interfering with concentration, the prayer of the heart helps us become more attentive to whatever we are doing by reducing unwanted distractions.[7]

Of course, we do not pray simply to develop more focus. We do not use the prayer merely to rid ourselves of unwanted distractions. We pray breath prayers and prayers of the heart to praise God and honor our dependence on the Holy One. Even our longing to pray without ceasing should not motivate our practice of these repetitive prayers. If we pray with any results in mind, we put ourselves and our own desires, rather than God, at the center of our prayer. With God at the center, our faithful practice of different forms of prayer will produce fruits of the Spirit. We may discover that our lives have more meaning, our relationships are more loving, or our hearts are more peaceful. We could become aware that our hearts are praying for us and that with no conscious effort we are praying without ceasing. These fruits of prayer come not from our own actions but instead are the gracious gifts of a merciful God in response to our faithful prayer.

It is but just that our hearts should be on God when the heart of God is so much on us.
—Richard Baxter

DAILY EXERCISES

This week's reading offers several forms of prayer involving your heart and breath, practices rooted in the ancient Christian tradition. Just as the rhythms of heartbeat and breathing are essential to physical life, so prayer is necessary to the spiritual life. Read Week 3, "Praying by Heart," before you begin these reflection exercises. As you read and complete each exercise, note thoughts, feelings, insights, and questions in your journal. Be aware of your heart and breath as vessels of prayer this week.

Exercise 1 Pray with All Your Heart

Read Deuteronomy 6:4-5. These verses give us the Shema (from the Hebrew verb meaning "to hear"): "Hear, O Israel: The Lord is our God, the Lord alone. You shall love the Lord your God with all your heart, and with all your soul, and with all your might." Christians are most familiar with this Jewish prayer from the Great Commandment as quoted by Jesus (see Matthew 22:37; Mark 12:29-30; Luke 10:27).

Practice loving the Lord with all your heart by focusing on the rhythm of your heart. Listen to your heartbeat; feel your pulse; sense the lifeblood coursing through your veins. Let your heart set a rhythm for your prayer. Repeat the traditional words according to your heartbeat: "The Lord is our God, the Lord alone." Spend five to ten minutes repeating the words of the Shema rhythmically so that they become emblazoned on your heart. Then write in your journal about the experience. For the next twenty-four hours, let your heartbeat remind you of your Lord.

Exercise 2 Adopt the Jesus Prayer

Reread the section of the chapter on the Jesus Prayer (pages 38–39). Write the traditional form in your journal: "Lord Jesus Christ, Son of God, have mercy on me, a sinner." Examine each phrase separately and consider the meaning for your life. Make notes on your thoughts.

Try saying the prayer in full. Think about the phrases you resonate with more readily than others and why. Then decide how you can best make the Jesus Prayer your own, revising or leaving out phrases that don't seem to fit.

When you are satisfied with your own form of the prayer, assume a comfortable position and spend five to ten minutes relating to God through the words of the Jesus Prayer. Close with a word of praise and thanksgiving. If you wish to make further journal notes, do so.

EXERCISE 3 CREATE A JESUS PRAYER

Read Luke 18:35-43. A blind man seeking healing cries out, "Jesus, Son of David, have mercy on me!" Notice the similarity of his request to the traditional Jesus Prayer. Use the blind man's words as a model for creating your own prayer. First notice how the man's prayer became the beginning of his healing interaction with Jesus. Identify a place in your life where you would like to find healing.

In your journal answer these questions: (1) What name for Jesus draws you close to him in prayer? (2) What quality of Jesus inspires you and fosters trust in you? (3) What request do you have for Jesus? (4) What description of yourself or your situation will make your need known? Your responses to these questions will give you the four essential parts of your own Jesus Prayer.

Write your prayer in the simplest terms you can. Spend a few minutes repeating this prayer right now. Take it with you for the next twenty-four hours as an ongoing conversation with God. Make yourself and your needs known to Christ.

EXERCISE 4 BREATHE YOUR PRAYER

Read Genesis 2:7 and John 20:19-23. Just as God first breathed the breath of life into Adam's nostrils, the resurrected Jesus breathed on his disciples with the Holy Spirit. In both Hebrew and Greek, the word for spirit also means wind or breath. In your journal write about the connections you see between these two passages and about what God gives Adam and what Jesus gives his disciples.

After recording your thoughts, focus on your breathing. Lie on your back and watch the rising and falling of your abdomen as you breathe deeply or simply place your hand below your rib cage to feel the expansion. Listen to the sound of the air rushing in and out of your body. Receive and offer every breath as a prayer. Consider turning the words of Jesus to his disciples into a prayer phrase to accompany each breath, inhaling the Spirit and exhaling your response. For example, "Holy Spirit, I receive you"; "Peace be with you, and also with you"; "As the Father sends me, so I send you."

Record your experience in your journal. Resolve to carry this prayer with you for the next several hours.

Exercise 5 Create a New Prayer

Read 1 Thessalonians 5:17. By now you have experienced a variety of ways to pray unceasingly, as Paul invites us to do. Recall your prayer experience thus far and this week's prayer exercises. What prayer words or phrases stay with you more than others? Which approach seems to fit you best? Look beneath the surface of the prayer forms. What deep need continues to surface as you pray?

You are now ready to develop your own breath prayer, a prayer of six to eight syllables that will fit easily into your natural rhythms. As a starting place you may want to use words and phrases that keep coming back to you.

Choose a divine name or image that may come at the beginning or end of the prayer (such as "Spirit of God"). Include a request that addresses your need ("give me new life"). Experiment with the wording until you find a prayer that flows freely from your lips. Write it in your journal. Sit with your prayer for several minutes. Let this become your ceaseless prayer for the next twenty-four hours.

Remember to review your weekly journal entries in preparation for the group meeting.

Week 4

Praying with Music

The small choir of an inner-city Denver church gathered for practice. They came into the sanctuary with joy and enthusiasm, sharing greetings and news of the week. I was there to witness the making of music and to discover from the musicians how their singing became prayer. They had many ideas: "I love the community we have formed," one man said. "No matter what is in my heart when I come to choir, joy breaks through by the time we are done," a young woman proclaimed. Another chimed in: "The words we sing ring in my heart all week, becoming prayer." The words of these singers helped me discover connections between music and prayer. My observations during the hour of practice deepened my understanding.

Sue, the spry eighty-year-old choir director, began vocal warm-ups. She sang notes the choir would mimic, starting slowly then speeding up as the variations became more complicated. Voices become more confident, tones stronger and filled with energy. The group was coming together in the sheer joy of singing.

As the choir struggled with a difficult piece, Sue offered encouragement. A tenor said to me, "She thinks we can sing anything." I could observe for myself how Sue's faith in them brought out song from the depths of their souls. At the end of rehearsal a woman summed up their experience: "Sometimes we're not great, but when the different parts come together and we hear ourselves among the others, the harmony of our voices is a miracle."

Whenever there is a resurgence of the Spirit in peoples' hearts, they tend to pour forth their prayers and praises in new music.
—Avery Brooke

Hildegard of Bingen, twelfth-century mystic and musician, believed the human voice was created for praising the Divine Mystery. She said, "The body is the garment of the soul and it is the soul which gives life to the voice. That's why the body must raise its voice in harmony with the soul for the praise of God."[1] Singing praises to God involves all of who we are in prayer, using body, mind, and emotion as well as breath and voice. Perhaps this is why another great saint, Augustine of Hippo, is noted as saying, "The one who sings prays twice." The next time you rise to praise God through song during worship, pay attention to your singing as a fully embodied experience.

Congregational Singing

Most worship services include at least two or three hymns sung by the whole congregation and often a sung psalm. When we raise our voices together in praise we are following patterns described in both Hebrew and Christian scripture. The psalmist proclaimed, "I will sing to the LORD as long as I live; I will sing praise to my God while I have being" (Ps. 104:33). The writer of the letter to the Ephesians urged members of the early church to "be filled with the Spirit, as you sing psalms and hymns and spiritual songs among yourselves, singing and making melody to the Lord in your hearts" (Eph. 5:18-19).

The singing of psalms, known as "psalmody," is one of the earliest forms of congregational song. Both Jews and Christians have sung the Psalter for millennia. In the style of ancient Hebrew poetry, the psalms express a great range of human emotion and spiritual depth. The book of Psalms has been called the prayer book of the Bible. These poems of praise and songs of lament give us permission to bring all our feelings into prayer.

The Psalms and other forms of religious poetry provide words for most of our hymns. Well-known hymn writer Fanny Crosby defines a hymn as "a song of the heart to God."[2] Her words resonate with me. Although I have a hard time following notes and staying on key, I love hymns and the opportunity to blend my voice with others. Some hymns bring tears to my eyes because of words or memories; others lift my spirits or calm my soul. When an old favorite is announced in church, I feel the delight of a child as I stand to sing, whispering to my husband, "I just love this hymn!"

All hymns are essentially the fruit of meditation.
—Avery Brooke

Reflect on your own experience of participating in congregational singing. What effect does the blending of words and music have on your spirit? Music by itself carries us beyond words and thoughts into the realm of feeling. But when music and words combine, our thoughts and feelings are integrated in a powerful way. Sometimes people feel the inspiration of worship most deeply through the hymns and anthems.

The purpose and popularity of congregational singing has changed through Christian history. In the sixth century, liturgical music was largely sung by the trained priesthood. In medieval times "hymns were used to educate Christians and to win new converts."[3] The Protestant Reformation brought renewed interest in the singing of congregational hymns, many of which were used to teach doctrine. It also reintroduced the singing of the Psalter into weekly worship.

The seventeenth century saw the advent of hymns expressing deep personal faith. Many English and Welsh hymns from the next two centuries are essentially prayers set to music. With Charles and John Wesley, hymns became "expressions of personal Christian experience."[4] American religious revivals and the distinctive strains of African American spirituals and gospel music have added their own flavor to our hymnody. In the last century we have seen a rise in hymns that address social concerns and a renewal of praise music in contemporary Christian worship. Congregational song is clearly an integral part of our common worship.

Styles of Musical Prayer

Christians have a long history of filling secular music forms with sacred content. Giving popular music spiritual meaning has proved an effective way to share the good news up to the present day. Many styles of music, from ancient to modern, can become vehicles of prayer for us.

Lifting our voices in praise through the ancient musical form of chant has become popular in many churches in the last twenty years, largely due to the influence of the Taizé community in southern France. Established in 1940 by Brother Roger, this ecumenical monastic community is centered around prayer three times a day. People from all over the world come to visit and participate in the community's worship, scripture study, and work with the poor. According to Brother Roger,

> Nothing is more conducive to a communion with the living God than a meditative common prayer with, as its high point, singing that never ends and that continues in the silence of one's heart when one is alone again. . . .
>
> Prayer is a serene force at work within human beings, stirring them up, transforming them, never allowing them to close their eyes in the face of evil, of wars, of all that threatens the weak of this world.[5]

Taizé chants, usually sung in Latin, may employ other modern languages. Because they are easy to sing, these chants have become an integral part of many church liturgies and find special favor in retreat settings. Commenting on the popularity of chant, Benedictine Brother David Steindl-Rast writes, "Chant is a folk art. Its imperfection is part of its perfection. It accommodates all kinds of voices and vocal skill. . . . And this is the point: A remarkable transcendent beauty is generated when ordinary people, with their shortcomings, give themselves to the chant."[6]

When words are set to music, it makes it easier to learn them by heart.
—Avery Brooke

When I chant the words, the music begins to move from my head to my heart, becoming a sung breath prayer. I may continue to chant the words to myself during the day, but sometimes the simple tune will arise spontaneously from my heart. As someone who has little knowledge of music and no confidence when it comes to singing, chant has offered me a way to participate in musical prayers. I encourage you to seek out Taizé services being held in your community. If there are none, many good recordings can help you discover the joy of chant.

Modern styles of music can certainly be forms of prayer as well. Music scholar Don Saliers affirms that country music "so often portrays the range of emotions we find in the psalms." A younger generation favors certain kinds of rock music to communicate faith and personal reflection. The current popularity of Celtic music comes in part from its spiritual themes and soulful style.

Recently I have discovered prayer in an unlikely place—hip-hop, which is contemporary music consisting of rhythmical lyrics performed solo or with instrumental accompaniment. Jamie, a young educator, writes and performs his own music. After hearing his hip-hop during a contemporary worship service in a local church, I sought him out to ask some questions.

Jamie's music expresses his passion for the gospel message of social justice. "When I experience or read about injustice, oppression, and prejudice, I feel angry and need a way to express it," he told me. "I sit down to write, and my ideas simply begin to flow in hip-hop style. I go back later and work them over to get the meaning and the rhythm right. I often think I am writing prayers."

"What about performing?" I asked him. "Is that prayer?"

"It feels more like prayer performing at church than at a nightclub," he laughed. "But in both places my music is a witness and a testimony to my love of God and my commitment to justice and peace." As I read his lyrics and listened to the music, I discovered many references to biblical language, gospel values, and traditional prayers.

One of my favorite pieces is "One Love," created for a interfaith gathering of young people. It begins with words that are welcoming and instructive about hip-hop. Jamie ends the first verse with this assurance:

> Lemme clear the air
> This is not a competition—Lord hear my prayer
> So if anybody listening is feeling scared
> I wanna make your spirit aware that
> You are not alone
> You are not alone

Next the chorus follows, in which the congregation participates. When Jamie sings, "One Love," they respond, "Agape." As you read the lyrics, try to imagine the impact these words and rhythms could have on a group of Christian, Jewish, and Muslim young people.

> You are (you are) not alone
> You don't have to do this on your own
> One Love! (Agape) One Love! (Agape)
> Solo it can feel like we're coming apart
> Together we're much more than the sum of our parts
> One Love! (Agape) One Love! (Agape)[7]

Hip-hop as prayer? What do you think?

Listening

Along with singing and chanting, listening to music can become a method of prayer. Remember a time when you intentionally opened yourself to a musical experience. It may have been a recording or a live performance. It might have involved a full orchestra, instrumental ensemble, solo piano, singer, praise band, or gospel choir. Whatever the musical form, were you able to surrender to the tones and rhythms, allowing yourself to be fully embraced by the music? Listening in this way with our hearts and minds is like surrendering to God in prayer. As the music surrounds and fills us, we are reminded of the wonder, beauty, and endless creativity of our ever-present God.

Listening to different kinds of music is an integral part of my friend David's spiritual practice. He shared with me his experience of listening to Gregorian chants while driving alone in the mountains. "The language was not known to me," he said, "but with the music filling my heart, I knew the presence of the divine." Listening to music also becomes prayer for David when language fails: "Not knowing what to say in prayer, I often turn to music, letting it express my longing for God when I have no words."

Like other forms of prayer, music can calm our anxious spirits, enabling us to be more attentive to God. When David played the lyre, King Saul discovered that he "would be relieved and feel better, and the evil spirit would depart from him" (1 Sam. 16:23). Whatever form of music calms your soul, listen to that music with your heart open. You may be surprised to discover that you are in prayer, listening to God.

Particularly when the turmoil in our mind is great, the simple tune and words of a spiritual song may lift [our] hearts and minds to a quieter plane.
—Avery Brooke

Listening through music to the Creator of all sound and harmony, we often experience a transformation of heart. "I listen to . . . music that can move me somewhere; it lifts me up, takes me to another place," Tom said when asked about the place of music in his spiritual life.[8] Tom is speaking of music's ability to help us transcend ourselves. Sometimes music moves us from despair to hope or from sorrow to joy. Sometimes it takes us more deeply into our sorrow, allowing us to lament with tears. Sometimes music stirs us to action giving us the strength daily to engage life fully and to work for God's justice and peace.

We pray by listening to music in other ways as well. A young woman once told me how hearing old love songs became prayer for her. She imagined the words to be an affirmation and expression of her love of God and God's love for her. Terry Tempest Williams, naturalist and spiritual writer, listens to bird song as a form of prayer. She listens to "the way their songs begin and end each day—the invocations and benedictions of Earth."[9] Listening to the birds reminds her of what she loves rather than what she fears. These little creatures teach her how to listen to herself and to God as they make music for the world.

Making Music

Making music with instruments other than the human voice can also be a form of prayer. The Psalms counsel us to "Sing praises to the LORD with the lyre. . . . With trumpets and the sound of the horn" (Ps. 98:5-6).

Judy has been making music since she was eight. Encouraged by her mother, she began playing the violin at school. At fourteen she was competent enough to receive her own violin and the instruction of a private tutor. Although she loved to practice and play, she realized she did not want to devote her life to becoming a concert performer. She wanted her music to be a part of her life rather than her whole life.

As an adult Judy understood how her classical training had wedded her to written notes on a page. She could not play from the heart until she met a group of fiddlers at a county fair. Intrigued by their playfulness and spontaneity, she recognized how her long years of lessons and practice had supplied her with both skill and inhibition. In order to play as the fiddlers did, she needed to free herself from the confines of her formal training and let her spirit soar. She took the leap and discovered the joy of playing from her heart. "That was when my music moved from the outside to the inside," she said. "I began to experience making music as prayer."

Years later Judy's experience of praying through music allowed her to play the violin at her mother's graveside service. She witnessed her music expressing her sorrow as well as celebrating her mother's life. Soon after, she began to play regularly at a local hospital's quarterly memorial service for those who had died in the past three months. "I believe the music helps others remember, grieve, and celebrate," she told me. "I guess it helps them pray."

Judy now includes jazz improvisation with other forms of music in her ministry. This creative process calls her to listen to the other musicians, blending her instrument with theirs, sometimes following and other times taking the lead. She read me part of a story that beautifully described her experience:

> [The woman] put the violin under her chin and, one by one, looked at the other musicians. Then, with a nod of her head that was almost invisible, the music began. Soft sounds from a guitar blended with the rich tones of a tenor sax. A drummer caressed cymbals with a steel brush. Through it all floated the thin, lilting melody of her violin. Together they moved through a realm so sweet, and sometimes so frantic, that it seemed to me they were all watching the same conductor.
>
> If so, no one else saw him. The four musicians stood alone on the stage, each adding what only he or she could to a creation that could not have happened without all of them.[10]

"What allows this cooperation to happen?" I asked Judy. She paused. "Complete self-responsibility and complete surrender—a humbleness of heart." Silent for a moment, I quietly said, "That sounds like prayer to me."

DAILY EXERCISES

This week helps you explore music as an avenue of prayer: singing, listening, making music both in and beyond regular church settings. Read Week 4, "Praying with Music," before you begin these exercises. Use your journal to record your reflections on both the article and daily exercises. Enjoy exploring the medium of music in your prayer this week!

Exercise 1 Sing Together

Read Exodus 15, which describes the celebration after God parted the Red Sea and saved the Israelites from the Egyptian army that pursued them. All the people sang and danced and made music before God.

Think about a time when you have participated in the excitement of group music making or singing. Write about your memories in your journal. How did you feel in the midst of the music? How was the music prayerful?

When you have finished writing, choose a song that serves as a prayer for you. Close your eyes and sing it to God, repeating your favorite verses.

Exercise 2 Listen Prayerfully

Choose a CD or audiocassette tape of music that you find particularly inspiring. It may or may not consist of church-related music. Listen carefully to one of your favorite songs or instrumental pieces. Reflect in your journal on what the music means to you and why. How do the words of the song or other qualities of the music speak to your soul? How do you feel while you listen?

Turn your listening into a prayer. Find a place where you are least likely to be distracted and can assume a comfortable position. Play your tape or CD again, listening to one song or several. Imagine that God is listening with you. Let the music be your gift to God. Don't be afraid to move with the music. Let your movements express your prayer as well.

Bring a tape or CD of one of these songs or instrumental pieces to your next gathering. Be prepared to explain to the group members how and why you find the music inspiring so that they may learn to appreciate it too.

Exercise 3 Sing from Memory

Read Acts 16:25. When Paul and Silas were in prison, they passed the time praying and singing hymns. They made their own music from memory. Imagine that you are in prison. What songs or hymns would come to mind from deep within you? List them in your journal. Sing one now for God's ears only. Hum or whistle the parts where you can't remember the words. Express yourself prayerfully through your music.

What difficult situation in your life calls for singing and praying to get you through? What song or hymn would sustain you? Try putting the words down on paper from memory; if necessary, look them up.

Conclude your time by singing your prayer again. Close your eyes and imagine singing your prayer in the midst of your hardship. Give thanks for the sustaining gifts of music.

Exercise 4 Play Your Prayer

Read Psalm 150. This passage illustrates that we don't need words to be prayerful. Instead, we can praise God with the music of all kinds of instruments. Spend ten minutes praising God by playing your favorite instrument or by using instruments available to everyone (whistling, humming, clapping your hands, slapping your knees, snapping your fingers, stomping your feet). Play whatever songs or sounds inspire you, or make one up as you go.

Whatever you do, do it prayerfully; lose yourself in the experience. Keep your focus on the wonder, joy, and awesomeness of God.

Set aside five to ten minutes at the end to write in your journal your reflections on the experience. Describe your musical expressions of praise. Consider what music conveys that words alone cannot.

Exercise 5 Compose a Prayer Song

Read Luke 1:46-55. Throughout the Bible we read words of songs, such as Mary's song of praise to God found in the Luke passage. Mary's song, known as the Magnificat, is her response to the Lord's blessing her as the mother of Jesus. What event or story in your life would you like to celebrate? What is the song in your soul?

A simple way to write your song is to create a brief response or refrain, such as "for his steadfast love endures forever" in Psalm 136. Simply tell your story with or without rhyme or rhythm. Then insert the refrain between sentences. Your song doesn't have to be perfect or beautiful—only truthful to your experience.

Let your song or refrain be your prayer today. Sing it several times to God with joy. Carry it with you through the day.

Remember to review your journal entries for the week in preparation for the group meeting.

Week 5
Praying by Gaze

For five days I have been by myself in a small house in the Rocky Mountains, gazing at the wonder of creation. High mountain peaks stand in the distance with soft, tree-covered ridges closer to home. For hours I sit in a comfortable armchair at the picture window watching clouds form, roll, and disperse as the sun moves across the sky. The aspen trees shimmer in the sunlight and respond to every passing breeze. Birds of all colors and sizes swoop onto the porch for bread crumbs while hummingbirds drink from the feeders.

In late afternoon the sky darkens and streaks of lightning cross the sky. The silence of the day is shattered by rolls of thunder, first far away then drawing nearer, followed by fierce wind and driving rain. As the forces of nature rage about me, I sit in awe of the beauty of the ever-changing scene. The sky clears before sunset, and stillness returns. I gaze at the sun sinking below the horizon leaving a soft glow that turns into a slowly darkening sky.

Gazing, Watching, and Looking

My time of gazing at the wonder around me is not the same as if I were *watching* the sky or *looking* at birds. Although gazing, watching, and looking all require eyesight, there is a subtle difference. When I watch, I am usually watching *for* something. If I hear a noise in the trees while taking a walk, I will stop and silently watch for what made the sound. When I wait for my friend to come for a visit, I watch for her at the window, looking forward to her arrival. "Remain here, and watch with me," Jesus told his disciples when he went by himself to pray in the garden of

Gethsemane (Matt. 26:38, RSV). Watching, while important, is not the same as gazing.

To look *for* also differs from gazing. When we have lost something, we look for it. We go from room to room, maybe to the back porch or out to the car, trying to remember where we have left it. When we find it, we experience relief and stop looking. We are like the shepherd in Jesus' parable who rejoiced when he found the one sheep that had gone astray (see Matthew 18:13).

To look *at* is still another experience. Usually we look at something to learn about it or discover a new facet. In art history class I remember our teacher telling us how to look at a painting: "Look at the colors; notice the brushstrokes; examine the subject matter. If you look closely, you will be able to tell the artist, the period, and the style of painting."

In contrast to watching and looking, gazing has no purpose other than to become aware of and be with what is before us. I call gazing "seeing with soft eyes." Soft eyes do not look for objects or answers; neither do they watch for the expected or the unknown. Soft eyes gaze at the world and see God in God's image, the Creator in the creation. When we gaze, we see with open hearts that allow love to inform our seeing.

Every prayer-filled day sees a meeting with the God who comes.
—Carlo Carretto

Remember gazing at those who are beloved to you? When you see them through the eyes of love, they are beautiful to behold no matter what they look like, and their presence fills your heart with wonder and gratitude. When I gaze at creation spread out before me, I recognize the gift of life and am filled with awe. My heart is open to receive God's love pouring over me. Gazing with soft eyes at others, the natural world, or works created by human hands turns our seeing into prayer.

Praying with Icons

In the Eastern Orthodox Christian tradition, praying with icons entails gazing with soft eyes at painted or sculpted images. My friend Liliana was born in Romania and grew up in the Eastern tradition. For her, icons lie at the heart of her religious experience and are not simply another way to pray. "I grew up with icons," she told me. "We had icons in our home, as did everyone else. In church we were surrounded by icons—behind the altar, on the walls, and above us at the center of the domed ceiling. The icons told us the story of God and created for us sacred space."

It was clear to Liliana from the beginning of her religious life that icons helped people feel closer to a transcendent God. "Icons are all about relationship," she said. "Since there is no way to know the fullness of God, we need a way to relate to the mystery. Icons serve that purpose by making God personal. Icons are understood not as depictions or images of God but rather as windows to heaven, reminders of the divine presence that we cannot see."

Icons are painted to lead us into the inner room of prayer and bring us close to the heart of God.
—Henri J. M. Nouwen

Artists who understand their task to be holy create traditional Orthodox icons. Their work is less about their own talent and more about their God. They spend much time in prayer and fasting before and during the creation of an icon. The figures rendered from both the Hebrew and Christian scriptures are not of natural size or proportion. Often noses are long, ears large, and mouths small. Hands are usually large with fingers elongated. The infant Jesus may be depicted as a mature or elderly man. The background for the figures is often a simple wash of color or maybe a landscape or rooms rendered in an unrealistic manner. This technique reminds viewers that they are not looking at the natural world but instead are being drawn into an entirely different realm.

For those in the Eastern Orthodox tradition, praying with icons involves more than gazing; it calls forth other actions. Because icons are so highly revered, the person at prayer lights a candle and kneels before a chosen icon making the sign of the cross and sometimes kissing the icon tenderly. "Westerners often mistake this reverence for an icon as a form of idolatry," Liliana said. "We Christians of the East know that we are not worshiping the icon. We are treating the image as we would treat anyone with whom we are in a loving relationship. Don't we bow to one another out of respect? Might we not kiss the photograph of a beloved grandchild? For us, icons provide a way to make a relationship with a mysterious God possible."

Liliana advises us to choose an icon to pray with that speaks to our hearts. She suggests we then find a quiet place, light a candle, and sit or kneel, if we are able, before our icon. Then we simply gaze at the icon with soft eyes while we open our hearts to receive insight and wisdom. Remember that gazing is seeing what is before us with our eyes and hearts. "Sometimes people will speak to their icons," Liliana told me, "and then they listen with their hearts to how the spiritual reality behind or beyond the icon might respond. Others simply gaze into the eyes of the image and enter into a heart-to-heart relationship. Occasionally someone will become so engaged in the loving relationship that he or she enters an alternative reality, and all else disappears."

Prayer is ultimately about being in love.
—Mark Yaconelli and Alexx Campbell

As Western Christians we have much to learn from our Eastern sisters and brothers in Christ. Let us be grateful for what we can learn and respectful of what we do not know within this rich tradition. Although our church buildings, liturgies, and traditions will not provide us with the full Orthodox experience of icons, we can to some extent recover the practice of praying with them. We might seek out a traditional icon or gaze at another image of holiness such as a favorite painting or statue. We gaze with soft eyes and open our hearts. Who knows what we might discover?

Natural Icons

Father Seraphim Rose, a twentieth-century Eastern Orthodox Christian, turned to the natural world for his icons. He taught that any part of God's creation could become a window to heaven, pointing the way to our mysterious Creator. Father Seraphim particularly loved trees and was known to bow down before them, sometimes throwing his arms around a particular tree. He was not worshiping the tree; rather, he was honoring it as a reflection of the wonder of God. He could also turn his attention to a single leaf, gazing at it for hours, allowing it to teach him.

As I was writing this chapter in my cabin in the mountains, I looked up from my work to discover a small rabbit sitting on the mat outside the sliding glass door. It was no more than six feet from me and absolutely still except for a slight twitching of the nose. This rabbit seemed like my own personal icon sent by God for me to gaze at and learn from. So I too stayed still, learning in my body and soul the pulsing stillness of a wild creature. I do not know how much time passed before the rabbit with simple grace hopped quietly away. I continued to sit, knowing this icon had been a window to heaven.

Windows to the holy are all around us if we will stop and gaze. You need not go to the mountains or the seashore to find a piece of creation with which to pray. A houseplant will do, a single flower, or a fallen leaf. If a park is available, you might stroll slowly, gazing at the colors, shapes, and movement around you. You might prefer to find a bench and sit to gaze at the wonder of the world passing by.

An icon is like a window looking out upon eternity.
—Henri J.M. Nouwen

We can also find icons in our ordinary surroundings. The city in which I live has numerous statues on corners or in courtyards available for anyone to see. Outside our library is a sculpture of a young girl sitting with a book in her lap and a dog at her feet. Gazing at that piece of art, I feel the wonder of children, the miracle of books, and my hope for the future. Some of the statues are more abstract; yet each time I gaze at them, I see an aspect that touches my heart in a new way.

One day I was feeling trapped in a city with no way to get out and enjoy the natural world. A wise man gently told me to open my eyes and see the wonder of where I was. "We often long for meadows and forests," he said, "and forget to see what is before us. Everything made by human hands comes from the stuff of God's creation. Our Creator is not waiting only in the wilderness. God is waiting for us right here."

Created in God's Image

"Right here" includes not only the environment of the present moment but also the people who inhabit our lives. Family, friends, neighbors, and strangers all offer us an opportunity to gaze at God. Scripture tells us that "God created humankind in his image, in the image of God he created them; male and female he created them" (Gen. 1:27). Therefore, when we gaze at others with soft eyes and an open heart, we can discover the divine in all whom we meet.

Thomas Merton, monk and mystic, was overcome by the way this view connected him to all humanity. He wrote in his journal: "Yesterday, in Louisville, at the corner of 4th and Walnut, [I] suddenly realized that I loved all the people and that none of them were, or, could be totally alien to me."[1] Later as Merton gazed at photographs of hundreds of individuals of all ages from many cultures and all walks of life, he exclaimed in his journal: "All those fabulous pictures. . . . How scandalized some . . .

would be if I said that the whole book is to me a picture of Christ and yet that is the Truth."[2] What insight! You may have had such thoughts yourself, although sometimes it is hard to see the holy in every person.

Gazing at the ones I love, I can easily see the holy shining through their very being. I know they are created in the image of the Creator, each one a child of God. But with some people I cannot transfer this way of seeing so easily, not to those I do not like or strangers I fear. Once I witnessed an altercation between a customer and a clerk in a grocery store. I did not see those two angry people as reflections of God. I simply wanted to run from the escalating voices; the angry, defensive facial expressions; and the possibility of violence. I lowered my eyes and shrank into myself, wishing the scene would go away. What might have happened if I had gazed at these wounded, vulnerable people and seen God in them, turning my gazing into prayer? What could I have learned? How would my heart have been touched? How might it have changed the atmosphere of the moment?

For a [person] of prayer is, in the final analysis, the [person] who is able to recognize in others the face of the Messiah and make visible what was hidden.

—Henri J. M. Nouwen

Many opportunities are present to gaze at people and discover God. The challenge is to practice this form of prayer with unlikely people. Who are the difficult individuals in your life? Are you willing to begin to see them as children of God?

A woman who participated in a mentoring program at a local state prison told me how she had come to see all the inmates—but particularly the woman to whom she had been assigned—as Christ. "I was so anxious and frightened when I went the first time," she said. "I wondered what in the world I had gotten myself in for as I was ushered through locked gates and doors. At our first meeting the prisoner seemed sullen and unwilling to share, but as I returned faithfully week after week she began to tell me her story—her history, her fears, her hopes and dreams. As our months together drew to a close I realized how she had ministered to me. She had broken my heart open through her trust, her words, and her shy smile. She had become Christ in my life. I pray I served her as well."

The Eyes of Christ

Just as Jesus teaches us to see and care for him in the stranger, the hungry and thirsty, the naked, sick, and imprisoned (Matt. 25:42-46), he models for us how to gaze at others with compassion. As I read the stories of Jesus' ministry, I like to imagine his gaze on those he taught and healed. I wonder how it would have felt to be among the crowd when he told us not to worry about our lives—asking us if we by worrying could add a single hour to our span of life (Luke 12:22-25). As I hear his words, I imagine him looking directly and lovingly at me. I place myself in the shoes of the bent-over woman whom Jesus healed in the synagogue. In this story he not only saw her, he touched her and declared her free from her ailment (Luke 13:10-13). Consider what would happen if we experienced being seen this deeply and truly? What might our world be like if we could gaze at one another—loved ones and strangers, friends and foes—through the eyes of Christ? Create an image in your mind of such a world and gaze at it with an open heart, willing to learn the wisdom it has to share.

Gazing at icons and the created world, seeing others and being seen through the eyes of Christ are all forms of prayer. Praying by gaze can be practiced in community as in the Eastern Orthodox tradition where icons fill churches and are part of the liturgy. We can also pray alone in front of a painting or by gazing at the created world in the midst of our busy lives. Gazing helps us attend to the holy that surrounds us in art, nature, and other people. Like other methods of prayer, gazing brings us into a deeper and more intimate relationship with God and opens the possibility of union with our Maker, the ultimate goal of the Christian spiritual life. Fourteenth-century mystic Meister Eckhart described this union in terms of vision: "The eye with which I see God is the same eye as that with which God sees me. My eye and the eye of God are one eye, one vision, one knowledge, and one love."[3]

What we are looking for is Who is looking.
—Saint Francis of Assisi

DAILY EXERCISES

Allowing the Spirit to open your eyes more fully through inward and outward gazing is the subject of this week. How you see what you see is a key spiritual practice. Read Week 5, "Praying by Gaze," before working through these daily exercises. Keep your journal close at hand to note feelings, impressions, insights, and questions that surface for you. Remember to stay open to the Spirit's vision as you pray by gaze.

Exercise 1 Seeing with Soft Eyes

Read Colossians 1:15 and 2 Corinthians 3:17-18. *Icon* comes from the Greek word *eikon*, which we often translate as "image" in the New Testament, as in "[Christ] is the image [icon] of the invisible God." Review the section on "Praying with Icons" (pages 60–62) and create a space where you can comfortably gaze at the icon of Jesus Christ on the inside back flap of your Participant's Book. Think about what it means to "see with soft eyes." Gazing on your icon can be a means of glimpsing "the glory of the Lord as though reflected in a mirror" (2 Cor. 3:18).

Spend fifteen to twenty minutes gazing. You may wish to place a lighted candle in front of the icon or hold it tenderly in your hands. Open your heart to the presence of God. At the conclusion of your gazing, take a few minutes to record in your journal what you glimpsed.

Exercise 2 Praying through Nature

Read Matthew 6:28. Select an icon from nature for your gazing today. If possible, create your comfortable space outside. Otherwise, position yourself near a window, a houseplant, or an image of natural beauty. To the people who gathered with him on the mountainside, Jesus said, "Consider the lilies of the field." In essence, Jesus invited his outdoor congregation to gaze at elements of nature in order to see more deeply the ways of God. Let the wonder of creation draw you into relationship with the Creator.

Gaze for fifteen to twenty minutes before writing in your journal. Describe your experience. How does gazing at nature compare to gazing at religious symbols? What insights have you gained through either or both of these practices?

Exercise 3 Loving through Gazing

Read 2 Corinthians 5:16-17. Since we are made in God's image, another person can become for us an icon through which to behold God's glory in the world. Find a photo of a beloved friend or family member to be the object of your gaze. Create your comfortable space and assume a prayerful posture with the photo in sight. Let today's reading serve as a reminder to "regard no one from a human point of view" but with the eyes of Christ behold the image of your beloved for who he or she really is—a child of God made in God's image. With this in mind, gaze at the photo prayerfully.

After fifteen to twenty minutes, answer these questions in your journal: What is the difference between regarding your beloved from a human point of view and regarding your beloved from a spiritual point of view? What have you learned through gazing about loving relationships? What have you learned about God and your connection to God? Record any further insights.

Exercise 4 Seeing through the Eyes of Christ

Read Matthew 25:40 and Hebrews 13:2. To practice gazing at others through the eyes of Christ, locate a photograph in a magazine, newspaper, or the Internet of a marginalized person or a stranger you might find difficult to love. Matthew 25:40 opens our eyes to see that we serve Christ as we serve "the least of these" with the mercy they need. Hebrews 13:2 reveals that we may show hospitality to "angels without knowing it." Use your newly acquired gazing skills to practice looking with compassion on strangers.

After fifteen to twenty minutes of prayer, spend some time journaling. What insights have you gained? How does gazing shape your attitude toward people very different from you? Resolve to see real people with soft eyes for the next twenty-four hours. Pray that God will send a stranger to you to help you practice seeing through the eyes of Christ.

Exercise 5 Gazing into the Future

Read Isaiah 11:6-9. Expand your gaze today by imagining the world as it could be. Today's reading describes an image of the renewed earth, an image commonly referred to as the peaceable kingdom, where natural enemies trust and live in peace with one another. Locate an image of a lion and a lamb or other natural enemies coexisting, or paint in your mind's eye your own visual symbol of the world God desires.

Gaze on your image of the promised restoration of creation; catch a glimpse of the possibilities. Let hope flood your soul; open your heart to the urgings of the Holy Spirit. How does gazing transform your vision? Enter your reflections into your journal, or draw a picture of what you see.

Remember to review your journal entries for the week in preparation for the group meeting.

Week 6

Praying with Our Bodies

With fear in his eyes, a young man approached me at the beginning of a retreat. He was holding a copy of my book *Praying with Body and Soul*, which has an image of a moving figure on the cover.[1] "You're not going to make us dance, are you?" he challenged me. "If you are, I'm leaving!"

You might have had a similar feeling reading the title of this chapter. I often encounter resistance when I invite people to think about and explore the various ways we can invite our bodies to be full participants in prayer. Many of us are uncomfortable in our bodies and afraid of how others may see or judge us physically. Some of us have had the unpleasant experience at some point in our lives of being laughed at or teased about the way we look or move, and we would prefer that it not happen again. We may express our dis-ease with our bodies by blushing when we are self-conscious, stuttering when we are anxious, or breaking into tears when no one else is crying.

God did not make us disembodied spirits. . . . it is through our bodies that we see and experience beauty, love, joy, and peace.
—Daniel Wolpert

The idea of praying with our bodies may also make us wary if we have never understood how our sensuality and sexuality can be a beautiful, healthy part of the spiritual journey. Remember in Week 1 how we explored the idea that God invites all of who we are into relationship? The One who created us good is interested in our full embodiment—our sensuality and sexuality as well as our thoughts, feelings, intentions, and actions. The mystics often spoke of their relationship with God in sensual terms. Sixteenth-century Spanish mystic John of the Cross likened the union of the soul with God to the marriage of two people. In *The Spiritual Canticle* he wrote:

> The bride has entered
> The sweet garden of her desire,
> And she rests in delight,
> Laying her neck
> On the gentle arms of her Beloved.[2]

For some or all of these reasons, you may feel a little nervous as we enter this week's discussion of the physical dimension of prayer. It may help you to remember that the ways you have been exploring prayer during these past three weeks have already engaged your body in prayer. You have been breathing your prayers, gazing at the signs of God's presence, and making music. This chapter will guide you more deeply into what might be called embodied prayer.

Embodied Prayer

Think for a moment of all the ways you use your body in corporate and private prayer. In worship you look at the cross, the altar, and images of our tradition. You hear the call to worship, music of all kinds, spoken prayers, and the benediction. You move forward for Communion or sit in your seat and receive the bread and cup as they are passed. You taste the elements and swallow. You raise your voice in song. You reach out to shake hands or hug another as you pass the peace. In times of private and corporate worship, your body is an active participant in prayer.

Perhaps in your personal prayer time you have discovered for yourself the best ways to use your body in prayer. Many people walk or swim while they pray. Others like to pray in bed before sleep. One of my friends gets back into bed in the morning to pray, sitting against a pile of pillows with a prayer shawl over her head. Maybe you have a special chair for your prayers, or perhaps you pray on your knees.

A creative way to think about the position or movement of your body as you pray is to reflect on the Christian tradition's six basic ways of being in relationship with God through prayer: (1) worship or adoration, (2) confession, (3) absolution or forgiveness, (4) petition, (5) intercession, and (6) contemplation. Each prayer form might invite a different posture. How could your body best express your love for God?

Imagine how you might move from a prayer of confession to a position of receptivity expressing your willingness to accept God's forgiveness.

A friend of mine created her own prayer dance by discovering a posture for each prayer form and then moving gracefully from one to another. "Sometimes I say prayers in my heart as I move," she told me. "I speak of my love, confess my sins, ask forgiveness, state my needs, and name those for whom I pray. But often I simply move slowly through the positions, allowing my body to pray without words. Praying this way, I arrive at my posture for contemplation easily and naturally and am able to remain in silent prayer for quite a while." In the privacy of your own prayer space, you might wish to create new ways for your body to participate in your growing relationship with God. In addition, start to listen to your body with love and open yourself to be guided into ways of prayer you have never imagined.

Express to God your intention to know God's love through your physical being.
—Daniel Wolpert

The main character in Sonny Brewer's novel, *The Poet of Tolstoy Park*, discovered while he was digging the foundation for his house that his body had its own way of prayer: "Henry let the shovel stand and lifted both hands to the sky in an attitude of worship. He lifted his face and closed his eyes, and suddenly, without warning, tears flowed from the corners of his tightly shut lids. He did not lower his chin, nor did he try to blink back the tears."[3] When words do not come, our bodies may shape our prayers for us. We stretch upward and weep; we dance in delight; we fall to our knees or lie prostrate on the earth.

Sometimes certain gestures can be conducive to particular attitudes of prayer. Do you fold your hands while praying, or do you leave them open in your lap? If not already part of your way of prayer, what might it be like to raise your hands above your head in praise or supplication? Consider holding a sacred object in your hands or lighting a candle during your prayer time as a reminder of Jesus' presence.

Sometimes our hands help us to pray in other ways. The most ancient branches of the church offer a long tradition of using prayer beads or rosaries to aid meditative prayer. But our hands guide us into prayer in other ways. We "pray by hand" when the work of our hands connects to our hearts, and our creation becomes an expression of love. "Hands to work, hearts to God" is an old Shaker saying. Author Sonny Brewer illuminates this phrase in describing Henry at work on his loom: "When

Henry wove a rug, he wove from the depths of his spirit and from the fullness of his heart, and with the careful eye of a focused mind."[4]

We might ask ourselves what we do in life with that kind of fullness of heart, depth of spirit, and focus of mind. Writing in a journal, repairing a toy for a child, knitting comfort blankets for the ill, or holding the hand of a grieving friend can become prayer as our labor rises from the depth of our spirits and the fullness of our hearts. Perhaps you are beginning to realize that praying with your body is not a new idea. You have been using your body to pray as long as you have been praying. You may not have paid much attention to it before, but your body is an integral part of your prayer life. Might you begin to think of yourself as an embodied pray-er, a "temple of the Holy Spirit"?

Temples of the Holy Spirit

Jewish tradition understands the human being as a body animated by a soul. In the Christian tradition we are taught that the essence of a human being is the soul, housed in the body. Both views recognize that the human person joins body and soul. However, in the Jewish understanding we are more a soul-full body, while in the Christian understanding we are more an embodied soul. In this matter, Greek philosophy has influenced Christianity more than the earlier Hebrew thought. We have placed a higher value on the soul than the body, at times seeing our physicality as an unpleasant though necessary cage for the soul.

Experiencing our bodies as vessels for the divine transforms our relationship with our bodies.
—Daniel Wolpert

The apostle Paul refutes a negative view of the body: "Do you not know that you are God's temple and that God's Spirit dwells in you? If anyone destroys God's temple, God will destroy that person. For God's temple is holy, and you are that temple" (1 Cor. 3:16-17). Paul clearly is talking about the human body, for a few chapters later he asks the community at Corinth the same question in a different way: "Or do you not know that your body is a temple of the Holy Spirit within you?" (1 Cor. 6:19). Knowing our bodies to be temples rather than cages helps us honor their unique ways of guiding us and participating in our prayer.

Honoring the Body

Caring for our bodies with love and tenderness can become a spiritual practice and a form of prayer. However, we often make the mistake of worshiping our bodies rather than caring for and honoring them as temples of the Holy Spirit. When we worship our bodies, we view them as all important, attending relentlessly to how we look, wanting to be admired for our appearance or physical prowess. Worshiping our bodies makes us guilty of idolatry. When we recognize this temptation, we may try to avoid it by going to the other extreme—ignoring our bodies or treating them solely as beasts of burden. Few of us have been taught to listen to the body's experience and wisdom. Usually we pay attention only when our bodies cause us difficulty through illness, accident, or aging. When that happens, we may often feel that the body has betrayed us, so we treat it as a problem or even as an enemy. How might we break out of these polarities of idolatry or disdain and instead treat the body with love and respect no matter its age, ability, or appearance?

Once, when struggling with my own physical image, I asked a friend if he liked his body. He seemed surprised by the question and responded, "Well, it's the only one I've got." His simple answer touched me deeply, shifting my focus away from concerns of how I looked to the wonder and the gift of my body. Like it or not, this is the body I have been given. It has carried me through life, and allowed me to experience the beauty of creation, the glory of love and friendship, the gift of growth and change. In this body I have traveled to far places and enjoyed the comfort of home, achieved success and failed miserably, experienced exhaustion and deep rest. My body has been broken and healed, has fallen ill and become well. I was born into this body, and in it I will die. My body is a gift from God. How can I not love and honor it, caring for it as I would an intimate friend?

> *When I look in the mirror let me see what You see—the self you gave me to be.*
>
> —Gunilla Norris

I have learned that to honor my Creator I am called to listen to my body and respond to it with love. As I pay attention, I know when it needs food and what kind and when it needs rest and exercise. If my body is hurting, I care for it tenderly, not expecting it to do more than it is able. In gratitude for all it has done for me I sometimes honor my body with small gifts such as a bubble bath or sauna, hot herbal tea, an occasional massage, or a vigorous rubdown. In deepening my respect for my body, I have become free to use intentionally my hands and feet and voice—all of who I am—to reach out to God not only through particular times of prayer but also through my daily tasks.

Action Prayers

Think for a moment of some of the things you do prayerfully. Do you tend your garden as if it were holy ground? Do you travel on crowded roads and bless the other drivers? Do you attend a business meeting with a desire to listen compassionately to those present? Do you serve a meal to your family with love in your heart? I believe that as we attend to the sacredness of our daily tasks, we not only do them prayerfully, but they become our actual prayers. Any action can be a prayer when, through that action, we turn our hearts to God.

Brother Lawrence, a Carmelite lay brother of the seventeenth century, practiced turning his heart to God and attending to the holy in everything he did. After a military career he lived for many years as a hermit. But in recognition of his longing for community, he later requested a place in a monastery in Paris, telling the abbot that his desire was to serve God and the brothers by doing whatever was necessary. He was sent to work in the kitchen where he attended to the divine presence in all of his daily activities. His way of being in the world became known as "practicing the presence of God," and Brother Lawrence soon became a spiritual guide to members of the community and to many others who came to visit.[5]

If we learn how to "see" and to "listen," we can make all of life a prayer.
—E. Glenn Hinson

Brother Lawrence also can serve as a spiritual guide for us today by calling us to remember and honor the presence of God in everything we do. I think that is what the apostle Paul meant when he admonished the early Christians to "pray without ceasing" (1 Thess. 5:17). He was not advising them to spend all their time in formal prayer but instead to practice the presence of God in every aspect of their lives. When we follow this teaching and turn our hearts to the Creator, all our actions can become prayers.

Quaker writer Douglas Steere illustrates this point with the story of an overworked missionary nurse in Angola who complained to her supervisor that after twelve hours on duty she was simply too exhausted to pray. Moreover, she had twelve patients yet to wash before she could go home. Her older colleague heard with love her anguished outburst and tenderly suggested that "if she washed each of these next twelve as though each were the body of Christ, her praying could begin at once."[6]

The idea of practicing the presence of God may attract us and touch the place in our hearts longing for a deeper relationship with the divine presence. But practically speaking, how do we go about it? I have discovered two practices to guide me: intention and attention.

Intention means naming my longing to be always in relationship with the divine. I can articulate my intention to honor my Creator throughout the day by saying a special morning prayer silently or out loud. I might write my prayer in my journal or use my body to express my intention. Some mornings I like to stand facing the rising sun and raise my arms high in gratitude for a new day. I then reach my cupped hands out before me as a sign that I am ready to receive the gifts that will be given. Next I cross my hands over my chest to remind me to take these gifts into my heart before I share them with my sisters and brothers. I indicate this sharing by swinging my arms from side to side at waist level. Then I press my hands together in front of my heart, bow my head, and ask God's blessing on my day.

During the day I can remember my morning intention by asking for the Holy One's guidance, help, and presence as I begin specific tasks. When I become anxious, I can remind myself that God is with me even in the struggles and find strength and renewal by using my breath prayer. Will my behavior noticeably change? Will anyone know I am praying? Perhaps not, but I will know that I am becoming more and more attuned to God in my life.

Attention lies at the heart of practicing the presence of God. When we were children our parents taught us to pay attention when crossing a street. Our teachers told us to pay attention to the lesson when our minds wandered. Our friends wanted us to pay attention to their ideas and feelings. We know the experience of paying attention to others, but rarely have we learned to pay attention to God.

Attending to God

If we are willing, God will teach us to pay attention to the sacred within daily life through our bodies. "Our bodies remain God's best way of getting to us,"[7] writes theologian and preacher Barbara Brown Taylor. How often when our minds and hearts get absorbed in anxious or driven concerns, God calls us to attentiveness. We hear the call of a bird and our eyes search the sky in wonder; we narrowly avoid an accident and exclaim without thinking, "Thank God!"; we visit a friend who is grieving and take her in our arms; we read of war in a far-off land and pray that those in the midst of violence and tragedy know the divine presence. In myriad ways our Creator "gets to us" through our physical senses, seizing our attention and reminding us we are not alone.

What reminders of God's presence do you receive through your body? What sights remind you of divine presence? What sounds, tastes, smells? How does the touch of a friend or the feel of the ground beneath your feet remind you of our Creator? Over the years I have asked hundreds of people these questions and discovered that virtually everyone experiences the presence of God primarily through their senses. Some will say nature reminds them of divine presence through a flowering tree, the crash of thunder, the feel of rain, the taste of summer peaches, or the smell of freshly mown grass. Others will name the things of church that remind them of God's presence: a favorite hymn, the taste of Communion bread, the smell of candles, the sight of the cross, the feel of a Bible in their hands. Still others recognize the presence of God in others: laughing children, a smiling stranger, a freshly bathed baby, a close friend, a longtime lover.

Listen to your life. See it for the fathomless mystery that it is. In the boredom and pain of it no less than in the excitement and gladness: touch, taste, smell your way to the holy and hidden heart of it because in the last analysis all moments are key moments, and life itself is grace.
—Frederick Buechner

Delightful or pleasant experiences such as these may easily remind us of divine presence and grace. But what about times of trial and struggle? Philip Simmons, teacher and author, reminds us to look for God also in the disappointments, difficulties, and brokenness of life. He writes, "The challenge is to stand at the sink with your hands in the dishwater, fuming over a quarrel with your spouse, children at your back clamoring for attention, the radio blatting the bad news from Bosnia, and to say, 'God is here, now, in this room.'"[8] Mother Teresa of Calcutta calls us beyond Simmons's recognition of God in unpleasant things to find God in difficult people and relationships. She encourages us to see "Christ, in his most distressing disguise."[9]

Try taking these challenges to heart. Practice saying "God is here" the next time you are assaulted by your neighbors' quarreling, see someone carelessly toss trash from a car, get drenched in an unexpected rainstorm, smell the pollution in the air, or bite into a mealy and tasteless apple. From his own experience Saint Francis of Assisi learned that the deeper lessons of God came when one embraced all things, even that which isn't beautiful. When we turn our attention to both delightful and painful ways God can get to us through our senses, we discover yet another way to pray in the midst of our daily lives.

I trust that by now you have recognized yourself as an embodied pray-er. You realize that your body is a full and active partner in your prayer life. You have seen how honoring your physical being and attending to the Creator in all you do can turn your life into prayer. You have realized the many ways God gets your attention and turns your heart to the Holy One through the amazing gift of your body.

To embrace the daily practice of incarnation is to walk the way of life that God opened up to us in Jesus Christ, by showing us how to inhabit our own flesh as fully and faithfully as he did his.
—Barbara Brown Taylor

DAILY EXERCISES

This week invites you to explore being an embodied pray-er. You already use your body in prayer and can discover many more helpful ways of integrating the physical and spiritual aspects of prayer. Read Week 6, "Praying with Our Bodies." As you read and work through the daily exercises, use your journal to record insights, feelings, memories, and questions. Stay open to the Spirit's wisdom as the week unfolds.

EXERCISE 1 PRAYING WITH THE BODY

Read 1 Corinthians 6:19-20 and Psalm 139:14. The apostle Paul calls the body "a temple of the Holy Spirit" and then advises "therefore glorify God in your body." Psalm 139 also recognizes a connection between body and prayer: "I praise you, for I am fearfully and wonderfully made." How long has it been since you thanked God for the gift of your body?

Take a look in the mirror. Instead of inspecting yourself for flaws as many of us are accustomed to doing, gaze on your own reflection. Be amazed at the wonderful works of God.

At the top of a journal page write the words *I praise you for . . .* in big letters. Now list what you appreciate about your body. What does your body allow you to do? How do the various parts complement one another? What makes your body unique to you? When your list is done, read it over slowly to see how your body glorifies God. You may think of new items to add to the list. Close by reading your list as a prayer: "Dear God, I praise you for . . . . Amen."

EXERCISE 2 PRAYING WITH THE SENSES

Read Isaiah 6:1-9. God has given us the ability to perceive the world around us in many ways. Explore the use of the five senses (sight, sound, touch, taste, and smell) in the passage that describes Isaiah's experience while worshiping in the Temple. What do you find?

Call to mind a worship service you have attended. Remember it with your senses by drawing a large five-pointed star in your journal. Put God in the center. Label each point with a different sense. Then fill your star with examples of how the worship experience engaged your senses. Observe which senses the worship service favored.

Go around the points of the star again, being present to life in God here and now through the exercise of your senses. Stay with each sense for a few moments in whatever way you can. Write about your experience.

Exercise 3 Praying with Leaping and Weeping

Read 2 Samuel 6:14-16, 20-21 and 1 Samuel 1:9-18. King David was not afraid to worship with his body as he danced with joy while leading the ark of the covenant home to Jerusalem in a procession. When his wife, Michal, objected, David defended his actions as a prayer before the Lord. In the second reading, Hannah seemed drunk to the priest Eli because she moved her lips without speaking aloud as she prayed her sorrow and distress. Our most profound prayers often require movement and gesture as authentic expressions of our true selves before God.

Find a time and place when you are least likely to be disturbed, and practice praying with your body. At this moment, do you identify more with David's joy or Hannah's distress? In the spirit of David, gesture with your body and hands in a manner that expresses joy in the Lord and, as you do so, find and express the spirit of gratitude and joy that is in you. In the spirit of Hannah, express with your body the sorrow and distress that you feel for yourself or for others. If other emotions well up within you, express them also to God with movement.

When your bodily prayer is complete, consider the experience. Record your thoughts and feelings in your journal.

Exercise 4 Praying with Posture

Read Matthew 26:36-39; Luke 18:9-14; Daniel 6:10-13; and Psalm 134:2. In your mind's eye, picture the outward postures of people in prayer. Make a list of all the outward postures you recall in real life, on television, in art, and in movies. Then review postures of prayer you find in the Bible readings for today. List what you find.

Reflect on the connection between prayer and posture. What difference do postures make in prayer?

Choose a prayerful position that is comfortable to you. Spend a few minutes in prayer in this position and offer to God whatever thoughts and feelings come to mind. Then try a less familiar posture, such as holding your hands upward or lying prostrate on the floor. Take some time to express your spirit to God in this way. Reflect on your experiences in your journal.

EXERCISE 5 PRAYING WITH ALL WE DO

Read Colossians 3:17. The apostle Paul encourages us: "Whatever you do, in word or deed, do everything in the name of the Lord Jesus." Everyday activities can be occasions for practicing a relationship with God. Think back over the last several days. Bring to mind one ordinary, common activity in your life. Reflect on what it would mean to do it in the name of the Lord Jesus as an act of worship done prayerfully.

Think through the next twenty-four hours. List the main activities in which you expect to participate. Close your eyes and visualize yourself engaging in each of the activities, whether enjoyable or difficult, as an offering to God, doing "everything in the name of the Lord."

Use a physical reminder (for example, a rubber band around your wrist, a string on one finger, or a small stone in your pocket) to help you practice remembering God in all you do, especially in the midst of difficult situations.

Remember to review your journal entries for the week in preparation for the group meeting.

Week 7
Scriptural Prayer

In the monasteries of medieval times the monks and nuns heard the Bible read aloud during meals. Most could not read, so hearing the Word was the only way they could become familiar with the poetry, history, stories, and instruction of the holy text. The readers read the words slowly and often repeated them, allowing individuals to listen with their hearts for the Spirit present in the words. I like to imagine those holy men and women taking in the words to nurture their souls while the food they ate sustained their bodies. Maybe they tasted the holy texts, delighting in the sounds and discovering the meanings hidden within. Maybe they savored the words of scripture as one might savor a delicious treat. I can imagine the Word, consumed slowly and intentionally, gradually transforming their hearts and lives.

Contemporary Christians can follow these sisters and brothers of earlier times and learn to pray with scripture. To pray with the Word, we will have to slow our reading so we too can taste and savor the words. Children know how to delight in words as they slowly learn to read. Watch a youngster with a book open on her lap, a finger on the page, intent on the task of deciphering a word. She will sound the word one way and then another, struggling with the syllables. Suddenly, the word she utters is familiar, and her face lights up with joy. She will go back often to read and reread the whole sentence, thrilled with this new understanding.

Scripture is a treasure; it sets the heart free; it brings light and peace; it is sweeter than honey and becomes like songs even in places where the psalmist is not at home.
—Elizabeth J. Canham

As children gain proficiency in reading, they begin to speed up. They race though stories to discover what will happen next. They skim textbooks looking for information or refuse to reread anything because, they say, "I've already read that!" Most of us carry these behaviors into adulthood; so when we read the Bible, we do it our habitual way. We often race through the words, searching for information, reluctant to slow down, unwilling to read a passage more than once. One of my students who was determined to read the Bible cover to cover before she started seminary laughed at herself, saying, "I've been trying to speed-read Jeremiah. It doesn't work!"

> *In prayer, as in the whole salvation story unfolded by Scripture, God is reaching out to me, speaking to me, and it is up to me to learn to be polite enough to pay attention.*
>
> —Virginia Ramey Mollenkott

To pray with scripture, we must break these old patterns and begin to read and listen in new ways. First we prepare ourselves to hear the Spirit in the living Word of God by quieting our bodies and minds. Then we choose a favorite Bible passage and read it over and over again. We might read the words aloud to taste them on our tongues and lips, savoring their meaning. If our imaginations are caught by a story, we can take time to place ourselves inside it and wonder about being present during the event. Reading slowly, we give ourselves permission to put down our Bibles before finishing the day's lesson when the Spirit catches our attention through a word or phrase. We might simply sit with these words for a while, carry them into our day as a breath prayer, or use them as a touchstone and reminder of God's presence in our lives. Reading the Bible this new way, we no longer read for information but rather with the intention of making the Word an integral part of our spiritual formation. This chapter will suggest some ways of breaking old reading habits so that you can transform your reading of the Bible into prayer, thus allowing yourself to be formed by the Word.

Lectio Divina

Lectio divina, Latin for "divine reading," gives us a structure for praying with scripture. Rooted in an ancient Hebrew tradition, *lectio divina* was practiced by the desert mothers and fathers and by later monastic communities. By the twelfth century this practice had been formulated in a pattern still practiced today. The monks and nuns were instructed to read or listen to a short passage of scripture four times. Instructions were given for ways to think about and pray with each reading. The first reading, *lectio*, was for the simple purpose of hearing the Word, which was rooted in the conviction that God addresses each of us personally through the holy text. The second reading, *meditatio*, afforded an opportunity to reflect on and ponder what was heard. The received Word was allowed to sink deeply into the mind and heart, connecting with thoughts, feelings, memories, and hopes. Next was *oratio*, spontaneous prayers of response to the gift of God's Word, whether offering thanks and praise, seeking greater understanding, or expressing deep feelings. The last movement, *contemplatio*, was time for resting in the Word and allowing it to rest in the heart. Led by the Spirit, words dropped away and the individual could simply "be" with God.

> *We will only be happy in our reading of the Bible when we dare to approach it as the means by which God really speaks to us, the God who loves us and will not leave us with our questions unanswered.*
> —Dietrich Bonhoeffer

I have found it useful to translate the Latin instructions into common English words all beginning with the letter *r*: *read*, *reflect*, *respond*, and *rest*. A Southern rural minister, hearing about the four stages of *lectio divina*, was heard to say that he had been praying this way for years without knowing it had a name. When reading scripture, he said, "I reads myself full; I thinks myself clear; I prays myself hot; I lets myself cool."[1] In recent years some have suggested adding a fifth step to these traditional four: *incarnatio*, or *return*. This final phase honors the need to put into action what we have discovered through the prayerful reading of scripture, to return to daily life assured of God's presence and more willing to love and serve the world. *Incarnatio* reminds us that the purpose of *lectio divina* is not simply to deepen our individual relationship with God but also to convert our hearts and minds to conform to the will of God so we may be faithful disciples in the world.

As you begin to practice *lectio divina,* you may sometimes wonder where you are in the process. You might discover that scripture invites you immediately into rest or that after you have responded in prayer your soul wants more reflection time instead. Sometimes you will find reflections and prayers interrupting your rest in the Word. All these experiences are of the Spirit and entirely natural; you may give yourself permission to follow your heart. People often move from the linear form of *lectio divina* to a more circular or spiral form as they become familiar with this prayerful process of reading. Whatever order you use, remember to respond to all five invitations. Many of us tend to forget or ignore the fourth step of allowing the Word to rest in our hearts. Yet, until God's creative word takes root in our hearts, it cannot bear fruit in our lives.

Reading Scripture Together

Although *lectio divina* was originally taught in the monasteries to help monks and nuns pray silently in solitude, a recent movement among laity and clergy alike encourages the practice of *lectio divina* in small groups. Gathered together around the Word, people often hear the stirrings of the Spirit, finding a richness in scripture they could not receive on their own.

> The following format is the one I use when leading group *lectio*:
>
> One person reads the passage aloud as others follow in their own Bibles. This *first reading* is followed by at least two minutes of silence after which another person reads, preferably from a different translation. In the silence that follows the *second reading*, I invite the group to reflect on what they have heard. Some questions to guide this reflection might include:
>
> "What have you heard in this passage that you have never noticed before?"
>
> "What teaching do you hear in these words?"
>
> "What do you wonder about as you hear this story?"
>
> After the silence I offer participants the opportunity to speak about their reflections. I instruct them to listen to one another with respect and to avoid turning the sharing into a theological debate.
>
> After the *third reading* and silence, I invite the group to pray about the passage. I encourage people to journal and often have crayons available if they want to draw their prayers. Occasionally someone will wish to move or dance to express their prayers. This private time with God can either lead to sharing or not, as the group prefers. I follow the *fourth reading*, the invitation to rest in the Word, with a longer time of silence—usually about ten minutes. After the *fifth reading* I give participants time to reflect on how the passage and their prayer together might guide them in their daily lives. These thoughts are shared briefly before I close the group with a sending forth and a prayer of gratitude for what we have learned and shared.

Each *lectio divina* group will likely discover its own rhythm of reading, silence, and sharing. If you create your own format or allow a structure to emerge organically from the group, be sure to remain true to your purpose—encountering God in scripture.

Some groups have a tendency to shift away from prayerful reading to a more familiar process such as studying the scripture, engaging in exegetical analysis, or arguing theology. One way to avoid these temptations is to include the imagination in your prayerful reading of the Bible.

The imagination helps to anchor our thoughts and center our attention.
—Richard Foster

Imagining the Biblical Stories

Whether praying with scripture alone or in a group, the imagination can deepen our prayer experience and lead us to new insight and wisdom. Remember in the last chapter how we attended to God with our senses? We can combine our awakened senses with our imaginations as we read the Bible and discover a rich sense of personal participation in the stories, making them come alive. For example, in Luke 6:17-19 after choosing his apostles, Jesus descends from the mountain to be met by a crowd:

> He came down with them and stood on a level place, with a great crowd of his disciples and a great multitude of people from all Judea, Jerusalem, and the coast of Tyre and Sidon. They had come to hear him and to be healed of their diseases; and those who were troubled with unclean spirits were cured. And all in the crowd were trying to touch him, for power came out from him and healed all of them.

This scene can be enlivened when the imagination begins to explore some interesting questions: How many people do you see gathered? Who is in this crowd—the sick, the faithful, the doubters? Who else? How does it feel to be among them? What sounds do you hear? What is the temperature? What do you smell?

As the scene comes alive for you, imagine yourself as part of the multitude. Would you be up close to Jesus or out at the edges of the crowd? Imagine why you are there and what you are looking for. If you are yearning for healing, picture receiving it now from Jesus. How does it feel to receive healing? You could end these reflections by drawing a picture of the experience or writing a prayer of gratitude for whatever insight or healing you may have received.

You can also use your imagination to reflect on what might happen after you leave the presence of Jesus and return home. Biblical stories rarely record people's experiences after an encounter with Jesus. We do not know what happens to the paralyzed man when he arrives home carrying his mat (Mark 2:1-12). How does the woman cured of a persistent hemorrhage return to her life (Matt. 9:20-22)? I often wonder what happened later to the one leper who returned to thank Jesus for his healing when the other nine ran away (Luke 17:11-19). Jesus' parable leaves us free to imagine what occurs within the family the morning after the father throws a party for the prodigal son (Luke 15:11-32). Using your imagination to continue or complete these stories can give you fresh insight into the meaning of healing, forgiveness, and celebration in your own life. Such insight in turn offers new opportunities for prayer.

If you wish to enter into a Bible story to experience what the characters may have felt, subtle movement can enhance your imagination. When you read the story of the bent-over woman (Luke 13:10-13), bend your own body, imagine the touch of Jesus, and slowly straighten your spine. In the story of Mary and Martha (Luke 10:38-42) read or listen to the passage while sitting on the floor as if you were Mary at Jesus' feet. Then hear the story as you stand in a pose Martha might have held when she came from the kitchen asking Jesus to tell Mary to help her. As you read the story of the man waiting for healing by the pool at the Sheep Gate in Jerusalem, lie on the floor and hear Jesus ask if you want to be made well (John 5:2-9). The wisdom of your body in conjunction with your imagination can deepen your scriptural prayer.

Ignatius of Loyola

Using imagination with a biblical text is not a modern method of praying. Ignatius of Loyola, sixteenth-century Catholic reformer, mystic, and founder of the Jesuit order, recommended this technique in his thirty-day retreat design called *Spiritual Exercises.*[2] Ignatius's *Exercises* were the result of his own spiritual experiences and his pastoral ministry as he worked with others, inviting them into their own profound experience of God.[3]

Ignatius wrote in his *Exercises* that "when the contemplation or meditation is on something visible, . . . the representation will consist in seeing in imagination the material place."[4] He recommended using all our senses to create the scene and then invited us to put ourselves into the story. For example, in the story of the healing of Bartimaeus (Mark 10:46-52) you might imagine being the blind beggar, feeling what it was like for him to call out to Jesus, "Jesus, Son of David, have mercy on me," then hearing Jesus ask, "What do you want me to do for you?" You might choose instead to become one of Jesus' silent followers or the one who ordered Bartimaeus to be quiet. You could engage the story by becoming one of Bartimaeus's friends who encouraged him to go to Jesus saying, "Take heart; get up, he is calling you." You might decide to enter the story in all four places, hearing with the help of the Spirit something different with each reading and discovering sides of yourself in the process.

We enter the story not as passive observers but as active participants.
—Richard Foster

Imagining the place and entering the story calls us into an encounter with the living God. However, as in the process of *lectio divina*, this encounter serves not merely to strengthen individual piety but to bring us more fully into the world. Ignatius of Loyola's spirituality was world-affirming and active. He guided his followers into scripture to make possible an examination of conscience, a conversion of heart, and a life transformed by love.

Self-Examination

The examen prayer, first developed by Ignatius of Loyola as part of his *Exercises*, is an opportunity to reflect on the previous day or week. We are invited to look for ways we have been present to God and times we have turned away. We remember moments of grace and wonder, as well as periods of sin and failing. God accompanies us in our reflection, comforting and protecting us as we examine first our *consciousness* and then our *conscience*.

During the examination of *consciousness* we pause to remember how God has been present to us and at work among us during the period under review. This is one way, as author Patricia Brown says, that "we heed the call to remember the wonderful works of God, the means God uses to make us more aware of our surroundings. God wants us to be present where we are and to discern the footprints of the holy."[5] The examination of *conscience* is a time to review our failings and uncover those areas that need forgiveness and healing. The words of Psalm 139 can guide this time of prayer: "Search me, O God, and know my heart; test me and know my thoughts. See if there is any wicked way in me, and lead me in the way everlasting" (vv. 23-24).

As Patricia Brown notes, the introspective nature of these two movements of the prayer of examen leads us to "the priceless gift of self-knowledge, not as a way to personal peace but so that we can resolve to be more fully Christian in our relationships and particular daily situations. It is not a journey into ourselves but a journey through ourselves so that we can emerge from the deepest level of the self into God. In this total, unvarnished self-knowledge we see our weaknesses and strengths, as well as our brokenness and gifts."[6]

Without knowledge of self there is no knowledge of God. Without knowledge of God there is no knowledge of self.
—John Calvin

The prayer of examen can be illuminated by scripture. The living Word can guide our introspection, shining a light into the darkness, helping us see what might be hidden.

Choose a short passage, such as: "Come to me, all you that are weary and are carrying heavy burdens, and I will give you rest. Take my yoke upon you, and learn from me; for I am gentle and humble in heart, and you will find rest for your souls. For my yoke is easy, and my burden is light" (Matt. 11:28-30).

Read the passage slowly, as if you were hearing the words for the first time. Then read it again, this time asking yourself how it might help you see where God has been present in your life. Use your imagination to return to your experiences of the week, using all your senses to help you remember. Maybe you will discover how you experienced an easing of your burdens or had a period of rest that refreshed your soul.

After the third reading ask yourself how these words point to a failing or a falling away in your life. Once, while reading this passage prayerfully, I realized that Jesus was offering me rest. I did not have to do anything to earn or deserve it—rest was simply a gift being freely offered. I had only to open my heart to receive it. I saw how many times I had closed my heart and turned away. I had not been willing to accept the gift and had instead gone through my days feeling burdened by my responsibilities. This insight freed me to reach out my hands, cupped to receive forgiveness and the lovingly offered gift of rest.

Allow the fourth reading to guide you into your next day or week. What is the lesson; what is the call? How does the passage help your resolve to be more fully Christian? You might write in your journal or draw an image to help you remember.

Ask God to make you aware of divine nudges in your life.
—Tilda Norberg

As you read through this example of the prayer of examen using a particular Bible passage, you will recognize elements of *lectio divina* in the process as well as earlier invitations to use imagination and movement to deepen your prayer. I am simply organizing elements discussed before in a different way. Scriptural prayer is of the Spirit—an organic process that will unfold as you practice the art of reading slowly, resting between readings, and entering the stories with all your senses alive. The structure of *lectio* and the wisdom of Ignatius of Loyola are presented here not to give you the *right* way to pray with scripture but to guide you into the wonder of the Word. Open your heart, and experience the delight found in the pages of your Bible. As you prayerfully enter the stories and poems, your own needs will be revealed and you will gradually find your own creative way to pray with scripture.

DAILY EXERCISES

Praying with scripture is central to the Christian life. This week helps you expand your repertoire of scriptural prayer with *lectio*, biblical imagination, and examen practices. Read Week 7, "Scriptural Prayer." Use your journal to capture insights and questions as you read the assignment and respond to each daily exercise. Ponder which of these practices you feel led to continue on a regular basis.

Exercise 1 *Lectio Divina*

Eventually, you will want to practice *lectio divina* on your own. For now, however, it may help you to be guided through the process. This exercise explores Jesus calling the first disciples.

Step 1: *lectio* (3–4 minutes)

Read Luke 5:1-11 out loud and let the words wash over you. Pause over any words or phrases that capture your attention. Be alert to your senses. What sights, sounds, textures, tastes, and smells does this story elicit? After you have finished this first reading, simply record in your journal the words or phrases that stayed with you. It's not necessary to write or reflect yet on anything further.

Step 2: *meditatio* (10 minutes)

Read the passage again, a few verses at a time and respond in your journal to the following:

a. Luke 5:1-3. Imagine the scene and Jesus' actions. Imagine Jesus getting "into one of the boats, the one belonging to" you, and asking you to "put out a little way from the shore" so he could teach from the boat. How would you react? In what ways has Jesus come into your life and used your "boat" for divine purposes?

b. Luke 5:4-7. Listen to Jesus' command to Peter as though it was Jesus' personal direction for you: "Put out into the deep water and let down your nets for a catch." Picture yourself going out into deeper water. What's down there? Let down your nets for a catch. What catch does God give you? Like Peter, call for help in pulling in your net. Who are your partners in responding to what Jesus is doing in your life?

c. Luke 5:8-11. Reflect in your journal on the call and the promise that you see and hear for you in this passage.

Step 3: *oratio* (4–5 minutes)

Reread Luke 5:8-11. Spend several minutes in prayer, turning your thoughts about the passage into personal conversation with Jesus. With the honesty of Peter ("Go away . . . for I am . . ."), tell Jesus your reaction or response to him and your feelings about who or what you are. Speak aloud and then listen to Jesus' response; carry on your dialogue as long as you need. Record it in your journal.

Step 4: *contemplatio* (3–4 minutes)

Read the passage again slowly, allowing the words to rest deep within you. What is God's gift for you here? As you experience grateful openness to God, leave behind attachment to everything else.

Step 5: *incarnatio* (3–4 minutes)

Decide on one small action that would serve as a token of gratitude, an acknowledgment in action of a single prompting or truth that you heard during this *lectio* exercise.

Exercise 2 *Lectio Divina* Revisited

Read Matthew 11:28-30 or Luke 13:10-13. Try practicing *lectio divina* using one of the two passages. Follow the five steps in Exercise 1 (above) or this simple description of the process. *Read* the passage for what you see and hear that intrigues you. *Reflect* on what the reading may mean for you or for where you find yourself in the story. *Respond* to God with your reflections, feelings, or questions; listen for what God wants you to hear or see. *Rest* in the gift of God's love. *Return* to being who God has called you to be.

Exercise 3 Scriptural Imagination

Read Acts 12:6-17. This passage is a delightful account of the apostle Peter's miraculous release from prison and return to the house where the church was gathered in prayer. Imagine yourself in the story by identifying with Peter. Read the story one verse at a time and write in your journal as you go. Describe Peter's thoughts and feelings, as well as your own at each turn of events. It is important to record your observations step-by-step because you will be experiencing the story as Peter does, without knowing what comes next.

At the conclusion of the story, look back over your notes. What have you learned about God by reading from Peter's perspective? What have you learned about yourself? Close with a brief time of prayer.

Exercise 4 Scriptural Imagination Revisited

Read Acts 12:6-17 again, and notice the role of Rhoda, the servant. Sometimes shifting perspectives can lend new insights. Rethink and reenter the entire story from Rhoda's point of view.

Imagine yourself in Rhoda's shoes. Record in your journal Rhoda's thoughts and feelings, as well as your own, as you read verse by verse. Imagine what Rhoda must be doing while unbeknownst to her an angel appears to Peter and sets him free. What is she thinking when she closes the door in Peter's face and runs back to tell the others what she has seen? How does she feel when she hears him knock again? Let your mind travel through the events.

When you reach the end of the passage, continue to let the story play out in your imagination. What happens next to Rhoda and the others who have gathered to pray? Write an ending in your journal. Then reflect on what her experience helped you see about how God is working in you. Close with prayer.

Exercise 5 Examen

Read Psalm 51. This psalm is a heartfelt prayer that moves through the process of repentance to forgiveness to promise and praise. Verses 10-12 help us practice an examen prayer or spiritual review of our lives in the past day or week. So prepare your prayer space and find a comfortable position.

Step 1: Read Psalm 51 slowly to let the words become familiar.

Step 2: Think back over the last week to remember moments of God's presence with you. Reread verses 10-12 as you call to consciousness your memories from the week. Record them in your journal.

Step 3: Read verses 10-12 a third time as an exercise of conscience. At what points during the week did you move closer to God? At what points did you fall away? Again, write your thoughts in your journal.

Step 4: Read the verses one last time with an eye to the future. What will you strive to do differently in the days ahead as a result of your self-examination? Make a journal entry to that effect.

Let Psalm 51:15 be your closing prayer: "O Lord, open my lips, and my mouth will declare your praise."

Remember to review your journal entries for the week in preparation for the group meeting.

Week 8

Contemplative Prayer

An announcement in the church bulletin caught my eye. It was for "The Sounds of Silence: A Contemplative Retreat." "Come spend the weekend in a small mountain retreat with others who long for silence," read the invitation. I was intrigued. I had experienced the blessing of silence when alone but never in community. Not knowing what to expect, I decided to attend. That weekend introduced me to the wonders of contemplative prayer. I discovered how silence and stillness could deepen and strengthen my relationship with God.

Contemplative prayer may appear to contradict the busyness and activity of our Western churches. Our worship services are filled with music and scripture readings, sermons and spoken prayer. If silent prayer is invited within the congregation, it usually lasts no longer than a minute. Bible study, service projects, committee meetings, and fellowship are our most familiar church activities. Solitary prayer among Western Christians most commonly involves verbal prayer forms such as reading a devotional guide or offering intercessory prayers for specific persons.

During the weeks we have spent in *The Way of Prayer* we have stretched the boundaries of our prayer lives so that our personal practices may now include music, images, words, and actions. We may not think of ourselves as contemplative as we sing, draw, dance, and enact our prayers; but the seeds of contemplation lie hidden in all these prayer forms.

Consider your experience of praying by gaze. As you let go of looking at the icon or watching the object of your attention, your vision softened and you gazed, opening to the possibility of being drawn into an encounter with God. If you practiced the Jesus Prayer or breath prayer, you may have discovered at some point that you were no longer thinking the words; rather, they arose spontaneously within you to remind you of the continual presence of God. When praying the scriptures you may have been guided to a deep place where the Word rested in you, and you were able to rest in God. In those moments you were being drawn into contemplative prayer.

Resting in God is a gift open to all.
—Thomas Ward

Contemplative prayer, in its most basic expression, is a loving attentiveness to God. We attend to the One who loves us, who is near us, who draws us ever closer. Words recede into the background and are replaced with a deeply experienced sense of God. John Wesley, describing his most profound experience of divine presence, wrote: "I felt my heart strangely warmed."[1] Others have named their experience of God in different ways. One man described it as a sense of disappearing into the heart of God. A woman used the phrase "surrounded and filled with radiant love."

Thomas Merton stated that "true contemplation is . . . a theological grace."[2] Author and spiritual director Avery Brooke, writing on contemplative prayer, goes on to provide vivid descriptions of this grace. Contemplation, she writes, is like a doorway and

> the key is on God's side of the door. Sometimes the door opens so slowly that we don't know that it is happening and are surprised when we discover the door is open. At other times, there is a sudden flooding of light or movement of the soul that is not of our making. We find ourselves in a place of great freedom, but it is God's freedom and not our own.[3]

Whatever words we use to describe the experience, contemplation comes as a gift from God, for it is not something we achieve by our own efforts. God's will, not ours, draws us into a realm beyond adequate words or images.

Two Ways of Knowing God

In the great stream of Christianity there are two ways of coming to know God. One could be called "the way of mystery" and the other "the way of revelation." The way of mystery, or apophatic path, points to God through the path of hiddenness and darkness. Along this path the Holy One is known only by "not knowing." God cannot be fully explained, named, imagined, or described. No matter how hard we try, we cannot comprehend the great Mystery with our rational minds. However, we can be drawn into a deep experience of this Mystery through grace.

We of Western Christian traditions are more familiar with the way of revelation, or kataphatic path, in which we encounter God "through the creation, light and sound, colors and senses, words and images."[4] All the ways of prayer you have been practicing these past weeks come out of this tradition. You have verbalized, sung, and drawn your prayers, discovering the loving presence of God through iconographic images, the steady beat of your heart, and the wonder of your breath. You have known your Creator in the wind and sunshine, the laughter of a child, and perhaps even in painful arguments with those you love best.

Although the way of revelation is more familiar, most of us have had mystical experiences even if we could not name them. That was the case for a woman who came to me with concern in her eyes after a session in prayer class. We had been doing guided imagery in which I had invited the students to imagine themselves in a place where they could perceive God's presence. I asked them to experience that place with all their senses—the look, the sounds, the warmth or coolness of the place, the feel of the ground beneath their feet.

In other words, I had invited students into a prayer experience in the way of revelation. We were using our imaginations to experience the presence of God. The other students stayed with the meditation, drew pictures of their sacred spaces after they opened their eyes, and then shared their drawings with one another, speaking of what they had learned. But this particular student was drawn beyond the way of revelation into the darkness and mystery of not knowing, the mystery of God. She did not understand her experience. "I closed my eyes," she said. "I heard your first words, and I went to a holy place in the woods. Then I went away. I heard nothing else until you gently called us back to be present in this room. What happened? What did I do wrong?"

"What was your experience?" I asked her.

"Peace," she replied. "A peace deep in my body and soul." We talked about the way of mystery, and it relieved her to know that her experience was a long-recognized form of prayer. She was filled with gratitude for the grace she had received.

The revealed and hidden ways are not in competition with each other, and one is not better than the other. They are simply different ways of becoming more intimate with God. Some people seem to be called to one method of prayer rather than the other, but all of us have experiences of both traditions and can appreciate them equally. As my student discovered, we never know what God may have in mind for us. However, we need not wait to be surprised by an experience of holy mystery, for there are contemplative prayer practices that specifically honor this way of hiddenness. Among these, Centering Prayer is one of the most frequently used prayer methods for contemplative practice.

One of the most profound forms of prayer is simply stilling our souls in the heart of divine love and waiting quietly for the Spirit to do its work.
—Marjorie J. Thompson

Centering Prayer

In the 1970s Trappist monks William Meninger, M. Basil Pennington, and Thomas Keating developed Centering Prayer—a way of praying based on the wisdom of the early desert fathers and mothers and two great Carmelites, John of the Cross and Teresa of Avila. Particularly influential in the Trappists' understanding of contemplative prayer were the writings of the fourteenth-century anonymous author of *The Cloud of Unknowing*. This guidebook of prayer, written for a young novice, is based on the theory that we can never truly know God by thought, for a "cloud of unknowing" separates all humankind from God. The only way to know God fully is through love. In the book the novice is instructed to pierce the cloud with longing and love. The author gives these instructions:

> Lift up your heart to God with a meek stirring of love, seeking God . . . and none of [God's] created things. Think of nothing but God . . . , so that nothing will work in your mind, or in your will, but only God. . . . You must then do whatever will help you forget all the beings whom God has created and all their works. Your thoughts and your desires are not to be directed toward them nor to touch them in any way, neither in general, nor in any particular case; but you are to let them be and pay no attention to them.[5]

These medieval instructions are accessible to us today through the teaching and writings of Father Thomas Keating. He outlines a method by which we can focus our loving attention on God by consenting to the Creator's call to us to be in relationship. We go to the Holy One asking nothing, expecting nothing, desiring only to love God with all our hearts and minds. Words are not necessary in this prayer, for as Father Thomas writes, "Silence is God's first language; everything else is a poor translation."[6]

The Practice of Centering Prayer

To practice Centering Prayer, select a sacred word, sometimes called a "prayer word," to serve as a reminder of your consent to God's call to relationship. Choose a word that guides you into the Holy Presence, such as *Jesus*, *Trinity*, *love*, *rest*, *Spirit*, or *yes*. Instead of a word, some people prefer an image—maybe a rainbow, a tree, or the face of Jesus. When you have chosen your word or image, find a quiet place where you can be uninterrupted for twenty minutes. Sit in a comfortable chair that supports you and allows you to stay upright for the period of prayer.

Begin your prayer time with a simple intention such as "I offer you this time" or words from scripture such as "My soul thirsts for God" (Ps. 42:2). Then simply sit, holding lightly the intention to spend your time in God's presence. Very soon, if you are like me, your mind will begin to wander. Many interesting thoughts and sensations will appear, distracting you from the Holy Presence. You might notice your hunger, physical discomfort, or fatigue; feel gratitude or grief; or get an idea for a poem or a project. Memories, pleasant and difficult, often arise to attract your attention. The news of the day and your reaction to it may surface. When this happens, simply notice that you are no longer present, say your prayer word and return to your original intention—to spend this time with God.

> ***In order to pray, you have to stop being "too elsewhere" and to be there.***
>
> **—Douglas V. Steere**

The sacred word does not serve as a mantra like the Jesus Prayer or the breath prayer. We repeat those prayers over and over so that they move from the mind to the heart and begin to pray themselves. In Centering Prayer the sacred word only serves as a reminder of your consent. Don't despair if you become distracted during your twenty minutes and need to repeat silently the prayer word over and over. Centering Prayer is not about "doing it right"—it is simply about your willingness to be present to God.

Centering Prayer is simple but not easy. It seems foreign to those of us who have been brought up to be active and productive. We can become discouraged after periods of centering when we feel that nothing is happening, when the prayer time makes us anxious and irritable, or when all we experience is boredom. But Thomas Keating would tell us to persevere. Centering Prayer is about spending time in the Mysterious Presence and opening ourselves to the transforming power of God's grace. Although we may not see results in the prayer period, over time we will experience the fruits of prayer in our lives. We simply may not realize that we have grown in compassion, let go of unhealthy patterns of behavior, or become more able to discern God's will in our lives.

Discernment as a Practice of the Hidden Way

We often think of discernment as something to do—a way to understand what God has in mind for us or a process of figuring out how to make important life choices. Understanding discernment in this way places it within the way of revelation, for it uses the mind, imagination, and will. I find it more helpful to think of discernment as part of the way of mystery where it is recognized as a gift we receive from God. Instead of a process, technique, or plan of action, discernment becomes a way of being, an openness of heart that calls us to live with all senses awake and hands unclenched ready to receive.[7] Wendy Wright, a contemporary spiritual writer, captures this understanding of discernment in vivid imagery. She imagines discernment as the "turning of the sunflower to the sun, . . . or the restless seeking of a heart longing to find its way home to an estranged lover. . . . It is being grasped in the Spirit's arms and led in the rhythms of an unknown dance."[8]

Have you ever struggled with making an important decision? You may have made lists of possibilities, talked with trusted friends, asked God for guidance, and still received no answer. Then suddenly, for no apparent reason, in the midst of your confusion and frustration, you *knew* what you must do. That knowledge came to you as a gift from God.

Like receiving the grace of contemplation (the deep experience of God's presence), receiving the gift of discernment is not the result of our actions and efforts. We cannot create a program for discernment, but we can practice ways of being, qualities of heart, and mental attitudes that allow us to be more open and receptive when the gift is given. We have discussed many of these discernment methods in this and previous weeks—practicing silence, listening with our hearts, honoring our bodies, reading scripture and resting in the Word, quieting ourselves with music, or gazing at images of the holy. These practices do not give us clear direction or answers, but they do prepare our hearts to receive divine guidance.

All forms of contemplative prayer, including discernment, invite us to surrender to not knowing and not understanding. Letting go of being in charge and figuring things out demands a radical trust in God. If we are not able to trust, the tug of the way of hiddenness may create resistance in our hearts. When this happens, we can begin to deepen our trust by taking small steps toward the Mystery, pausing to reflect on how God's loving and trustworthy presence has been made known in our lives.

When we go into God's presence it must be a surrender.
—Russell Maltby

You might remember a time when you felt held by love or a time when you turned in an unexpected direction to find something you did not even know you were seeking. You could remember a longing that prompted you to take a risky step, or a time when all your senses let you know God was with you. These experiences will help you trust that God is with you and for you, offering loving guidance when you willingly open your heart and surrender to the contemplative life.

The Contemplative Life

The contemplative life is available to all who seek to love and serve God. Just as contemplative prayer is a loving attentiveness to the Holy One, so in the contemplative life we gratefully attend to the One who is at the center of all we are and all we do. The contemplative life will honor the way of mystery, including the practice of contemplative prayer; but it will not exclude other ways of prayer or ignore our call to love and service. People often mistakenly understand the contemplative life as consisting only of silence, self-denial, and retreat from the world when in fact contemplation invites our involvement in the world. We practice silence so we will know what needs to be said and how to speak the truth in love. We deny ourselves excess so that others may partake of God's bounty.

We retreat so that our reentry brings with it a clarity about who and whose we are that we might serve others with courage and compassion.

Years ago I attended a conference where Thomas Keating spoke about Centering Prayer. I was asked to be on a panel to respond to his teachings. When my turn came to speak, I prefaced my remarks with the disclaimer, "I am not a contemplative, but. . . ." Later a good friend asked me what I had meant by that statement. I told her that I didn't have a faithful practice of contemplative prayer, that I couldn't sit still, that I preferred to dance my prayers and was actively involved in issues relating to justice and peace. "You are holding a stereotypical image of what it means to be a contemplative and to live a contemplative life," she replied. "You need to rethink this."

We are spiritual creatures with the power of communion with God, breathing the air of eternity.
—Evelyn Underhill

In the years since that exchange I have come to realize that I am a contemplative involved in a contemplative life. I may not look or behave like others who claim the same identity, but I know that in my own ways I strive to place God at the foreground of my life, allowing other concerns to fade to the background. I try to live in gratitude to the Creator for everyone and everything in my life. I still do not have a regular practice of contemplative prayer, but I try to keep my hands unclenched and my heart open, ready to receive whatever God has to offer. Although I do not fit many people's understanding of what it means to be a contemplative, I know I am living a contemplative life. The contemplative life beckons all of us. Whatever prayer methods you practice, however many times you turn away from God, pay attention to your longings and consider whether you too are willing to live a contemplative life.

DAILY EXERCISES

The contemplative side of prayer, following in "the way of mystery," is one you may struggle to cultivate. Yet such prayer can be the root of deep healing, insight, and fruitfulness in your personal growth and Christian discipleship. Read Week 8, "Contemplative Prayer," then work through the daily exercises below. Remember to reflect on your feelings, thoughts, and questions in your journal. Open yourself to the gift and grace of the Spirit's hidden work deep within you.

Exercise 1 On the Threshold

Read Matthew 7:7-11. Especially consider verse 7, "Knock, and the door will be opened for you." Draw a picture of a door with you on one side and God on the other. Meditate on Avery Brooke's comment on page 96 that the key is on God's side of the door. On your side, jot down words that describe what desire, fear, or anticipation you bring. On God's side, write words that describe what you imagine that God desires, feels, knows, or is doing.

Close your eyes, and approach the door. You can't see beyond the door, but you know intuitively that God is waiting on the other side. What do you sense as you approach God's mystery? Knock. Ask. Invite God to open the door. Wait for a time in love and silence. Record in your journal what happens.

Exercise 2 In Trust

Read Psalm 33:20-22; 37:3-4; 62:7-8; 91:1-2. Trusting God, a key concept in the psalms, is also a key to the spiritual life. In your journal, create two columns. Label one side "Trusting Moments" and the other side "Distrustful Moments." Read today's verses one at a time. Pause after each to record in your journal life events that reflect either trust in God or difficulty trusting God. Interspersing your scripture readings with writing may remind you of instances in one column or the other.

When you have finished, take some time to reflect on your experience of trusting God. Over your lifetime, what factors have made trust possible for you? What obstacles have interfered with your ability to trust? What do you think would help you to become more trusting?

Pray the words of Psalm 91:2: "My refuge and my fortress; my God, in whom I trust." Memorize the words. In silence, trust your life entirely to God's care. Stay focused by returning again and again to the words of the psalm. As worrisome parts of your life come to mind, offer them to God. Continue to practice trusting your whole life to God in this way for as long as you need.

Exercise 3 In Secret

Read Matthew 6:5-6. In your journal, turn back to the picture of the door from Daily Exercise 1. Jesus says, "Whenever you pray, go into your room and shut the door and pray to your Father who is in secret; and your Father who sees in secret will reward you." Visualize a secret, sacred place beyond the door into which God has invited you. Imagine yourself sitting in God's secret, sacred place. Stay there for a while and be open to what may transpire between you and God in secret.

What do you see, and what does God see? What do you say, and what does God say? What do you feel, and what does God feel? What do you experience, sense, intuit? What does God reveal?

Remain silent for some time. Then thank God for opening the door to you. Be sure to write about your vision in your journal.

Exercise 4 In the Center

Read 1 John 4:16-19. In the hymn "Love Divine, All Loves Excelling," Charles Wesley proclaims, "Jesus, thou art all compassion, pure, unbounded love thou art." Consider the mystery of "pure, unbounded love." Choose a sacred word or image for your Centering Prayer. Remember that the purpose of this word is to call you back when you become distracted. This week's reading offers suggestions for sacred words or images (page 99). When you've selected a sacred word or image, write it in your journal.

Prepare your prayer space and assume a comfortable posture. Begin your prayer time with your sacred word or image. Spend twenty minutes sitting quietly in God's presence. As your prayer time ends, be sure to express gratitude. Then record any insights in your journal.

Exercise 5 In Need

Read Psalm 130. For a discernment prayer, begin by exploring a few of your deep needs that only God can understand and fulfill. Locate those places in your soul that resonate with the psalmist's prayer, "Out of the depths I cry to you, O Lord." Journal briefly about the deepest need you recognize within your soul and choose a sacred word or image that reflects God's ability to provide—*healer*, *lover*, or *friend*, for example.

Begin your twenty minutes of silent prayer time by saying, "I wait for the Lord, my soul waits." Remember to use your sacred word or image to call your mind back from distraction. At the close of your prayer, offer words of trust and praise. Record in your journal any discernment you may have received.

Remember to review your journal entries for the week in preparation for the group meeting.

CENTERING PRAYER SUMMARY

Centering Prayer is a method of contemplative prayer—a way of opening our whole being to the mystery of God beyond thoughts, words, and emotions. Contemplative prayer is a gift of the Spirit, not something we can make happen. Yet through grace we can open ourselves to God who we know by faith is within us, closer than breathing, closer than choosing, closer than consciousness itself.

Centering Prayer prepares us to receive this gift. It moves us beyond conversation with Christ to communion with God. The focus is deepening our relationship with the living, Triune God.

Centering Prayer Guidelines

Choose a sacred word as the symbol of your intention to consent to God's presence and action within. Select this word in a brief period of prayer, asking the Spirit to inspire you. Examples: *God, Jesus, Abba, Light, Love, Peace, Be Still, Trust, Faith, Yes.*

Sitting comfortably with eyes closed, settle briefly and silently breathe your sacred word as the symbol of your consent to God's presence and action within. Introduce your word very gently, as if you were laying a feather on cotton. Let it carry into a sense of God's real presence.

When thoughts come, as they inevitably will, return ever-so-gently to the sacred word. "Thoughts" in this case include concepts, reflections, feelings, images, memories, plans, and sensory perceptions or body sensations. Do not try to push thoughts away, simply return your attention to the sacred word and God's presence within.

At the end of the prayer period (20 minutes), remain in silence with eyes closed for a few minutes. You might wish to say the Lord's Prayer.

Practical Points

Centering Prayer is not a technique but a way of cultivating a relationship with God. Recommended practice is two 20-minute periods daily.

It is not a substitute for other forms of prayer but offers a way of "resting in God."

We do not analyze or judge our experience; nor do we aim at specific goals like having no thoughts, feeling peaceful, repeating the sacred word continually, or achieving a spiritual experience.

The fruits of this prayer are experienced in daily life, not in the prayer period.

These guidelines are adapted from the Contemplative Outreach website,
www.centeringprayer.com/methodcp.htm

Week 9

Praying with and for Others

My entering seminary in my early forties was not a response to a call to ministry. I went to study my Christian roots and heritage. I realized that in searching for ways to live and express my spiritual longings, I had ignored the tradition in which I had been brought up. Despite my active involvement in a church community during childhood and adolescence, in my early forties I did not want to join a congregation. I imagined myself to be on a solitary journey, independently seeking ways to develop my relationship with God.

Attending seminary meant that I joined a community of sorts, but I resisted becoming involved, keeping myself on the margins and shielding myself from others. One day as I studied alone in the library, a classmate I did not know well sat down beside me. I was annoyed at her intrusion, but she simply sat until I gave her my full attention. She looked me in the eye and said gently, "You know, Jane, you can't be a Christian alone." I stared at her in astonishment. She patted my hand, smiled kindly, then got up and walked away.

Whenever we pray, we pray with the whole people of God.
—Roberta C. Bondi

I did not want to believe her, but deep inside I knew she was right. Jesus said, "Where two or three are gathered in my name, I am there among them" (Matt. 18:20). Jesus calls us into community, into relationship with others as well as with himself and his Abba. When he taught the disciples to pray he gave them plural words: *Our* Father, give *us* this day, forgive *us* as *we* forgive, lead *us*, deliver *us* (paraphrase, Matt. 6:9-13). The wording of the Lord's Prayer reminds us that in truth we never pray alone but only as disciples joined with others in the mind and heart of Christ.

However, right before Jesus taught this prayer he reminded his followers to pray privately: "'And whenever you pray, do not be like the hypocrites; for they love to stand and pray in the synagogues and at the street corners, so that they may be seen by others. . . . But whenever you pray, go into your room and shut the door and pray to your Father who is in secret'" (Matt. 6:5-6). Some of us may have taken these words too literally, becoming reluctant to pray in community or even talk with others about our experiences of prayer. Maybe we worry about seeming boastful and proud if we speak of our prayer lives. Maybe we fear that our prayer life is inadequate, and we would be ashamed to reveal to others how shallow it seems. But can you imagine what might happen if we overcame these anxieties and began to share our prayer lives honestly and tenderly with one another—praying together and discussing our questions, concerns, and joys? We would begin to transform our churches into houses of prayer (see Mark 11:17).

Praying Congregations

Praying together can be a source of great comfort and joy. It is one of the reasons we go to church for common worship. Praying the memorized prayers of our tradition, reading a prayer of confession aloud together, hearing the pastor offer prayers for the people, and silently praying together as the body of Christ—these practices connect us and remind us we are not alone. The prayers offered during services of Holy Communion touch our hearts even as the bread and the cup touch our lips. Yet I invite us to stretch beyond those formal prayer times to recognize all of worship as a prayer. Let's think about the many opportunities for prayer we encounter in worship.

Attending worship can be a prayer of intention and consecration. We decide to focus our attention on God in the company of others for the length of the service. Other reasons for going to church may be present as well, but they do not negate the intention to worship God. Arriving at church, you most likely greet people—sharing a handshake, a few words, maybe a hug. Reaching out to sisters and brothers can be a form of prayer as we perceive each one created in God's image and recognize them as part of the body of Christ. The announcement of church activities and sharing of joys and concerns can be heard as God's call to service and intercession. Raising our voices in song, listening to the choir, and hearing the instrumental offertory all give us the opportunity to participate in musical prayer.

Hearing the word of God read aloud invites us to engage prayerfully the scripture as we open our minds to the insights contained within the passage. The prayer for illumination invokes the grace of the Holy Spirit to prepare our hearts to listen to what one person will say to draw us more fully into the day's lesson. When the sermon has been prayerfully prepared and the preacher is open to the movement of the Spirit, offering and receiving the spoken word can become part of our prayer. Finally, sent forth from worship with words of blessing, we are reminded that created by God, sustained by Christ, and inspired by the Holy Spirit we are called to love and serve the world. Our common worship becomes continual prayer as we recognize the abiding relationship with God underlying all its movements.

These liturgical opportunities for prayer are such an integral part of our Christian tradition that we can scarcely imagine a life of faith without them. At the same time, they are not the only ways to pray together. Our discovery of other ways to pray in community can help us become a praying congregation in a deeper and more comprehensive sense.

For most of Christian history, the prayer practice at the heart of all prayer practices was the church, and community was at the core of spiritual experience.
—Daniel Wolpert

In a praying congregation prayer becomes central to the whole life of the community. Members not only pray together during worship services, begin meetings with prayer, and dismiss gatherings with a blessing; they also talk about prayer, ask others to pray with and for them, form small groups to pray together, and encourage individuals to discover and practice new ways to pray. No one is an expert in a praying congregation, for all are exploring prayer together. One person may teach a class on a prayer method he or she has found helpful and another lead a group in discussing a classic or contemporary book on prayer. Someone else may organize a prayer retreat or invite a person from another faith to talk about his or her experience of prayer. In a praying congregation no one is afraid to raise a question regarding prayer, express doubts about prayer, or share an experience of prayer. In a praying congregation we would not be surprised to hear one friend ask another, "And how was your prayer life this week?"

Sometimes all it takes for a church to become a praying congregation is for a core group of people to begin making prayer a priority. Your

Companions group has done just that by choosing to spend ten weeks together studying *The Way of Prayer*, practicing different prayer forms, and sharing experiences. I imagine you have become comfortable expressing your doubts, naming your preferences for certain methods, asking hard questions of one another, and learning to live into the mystery of prayer. Some of you may have learned to pray aloud comfortably for the first time. When your time together as a group ends you might consider continuing to meet to pray together. In addition, some of you may be willing to reach out to others in and beyond the congregation by inviting them to join a small prayer group.

Prayer Groups

Think of one of the prayer forms you have experienced in the last several weeks that you would like to make part of your regular prayer practice. Would you be willing to ask a few people to join you in this way of prayer? Maybe you could begin a noontime *lectio divina* group and see if people will commit to this practice for a period of time, such as four or six weeks. You might let the liturgical year guide you, holding your prayer group during Lent or Advent. One church decided to give up all meetings for Lent one year. This decision freed busy people to join one of three groups studying and practicing intercessory prayer. The groups were held weekly at different times to accommodate a variety of schedules—early morning, noon, and evening. More people participated in these small groups than ever before because the church created time and space to allow for such participation.

The container of community offers safe space within which a group of people can give themselves over to God.
—Daniel Wolpert

As you know from your own *Companions* class, group members that pray together can become close. They know one another well enough to feel safe in being honest and vulnerable. Prayer times become increasingly meaningful, and conversation deepens. If you are part of a group like this that has completed its course of study, you may wish to continue meeting using another resource for guidance.

Other times, even when the members have become close, a group will know that the time together is complete. The participants can recognize the goodness of what they have shared and express sadness at its ending without trying to continue a group whose natural life is over. An ending can be a blessing by giving space for new groups to begin, creating an ebb and flow in the prayer life of the congregation. Leaders and members of the groups will change periodically; new methods of prayer will be introduced; and the structure and design of groups will vary.

Some prayer groups are held during adult education time on Sunday morning. You might provide a class where people simply have a chance to talk about prayer. Begin by inviting people to share how and when they learned to pray. In another session discuss what beliefs they hold about prayer, encouraging both the sharing of personal convictions and respect for differences. Later you might help them reflect on how they imagine the God to whom they pray. A class like this will allow its members to voice questions they may never have had the opportunity to ask.

If people in your church prefer to study a topic rather than engage in personal discussion, gather a group to read and study a book on prayer. Another idea is to hold a class series with different members of the congregation teaching methods of prayer they practice on their own or with a group. This class structure allows people to realize how many different forms of prayer are being practiced within their congregation, as well as encouraging a wide variety of leadership.

One urban church holds a thirty-minute session of Centering Prayer one morning a week. The pastor, who had been practicing Centering Prayer on his own for many years, wanted to practice with a group and afforded the opportunity to the church. It was not a class or a discussion group, and the membership was always open. The pastor told me a small core of people attended faithfully; others came for a while and then disappeared; and some just dropped in every now and then. "The interesting thing," he said, "is how many people who don't join us tell me they find comfort in just knowing we are praying. Somehow they become partners in prayer."

Prayer Partners

There are formal ways to become prayer partners. Two people may agree to pray for each other every day. Such partners may live close by or far away. Some churches encourage the pairing of senior adults and

A spiritual guide is someone who can help us see and name our own experience of God.
—Marjorie J. Thompson

teenagers, a valuable connection for both that may not occur in any other way. These prayer partners may speak or visit with each other periodically, but the primary commitment is to pray consistently for the other. If you have ever had the blessing of knowing you were being prayed for daily, you know the power of this type of partnering.

Another model for partnering involves two people meeting at a specific and regular time to pray together. They may decide to practice a form of silent prayer, pray scripture together, pray aloud for each other, listen to sacred music, or participate in a combination of practices. Sometimes praying is all they do together, but often prayer partners begin to talk about their experiences of prayer or the effects of prayer in their lives. As prayer partners begin to share, they often realize they have become spiritual friends, or soul friends (a guide, mentor, or support to us as we mature in Christ). Sometimes people begin a relationship as soul friends and then decide to become prayer partners.

Lauren Winner, author and memoirist, shares a story about her prayer partner and soul friend who kept her faithful to body prayer. The two women agreed to meet at an exercise class. She writes:

> I must confess there are only two reasons I get up for my 7:30 exercise class: the knowledge that my friend Molly is there and will kill me if I don't show up, and the equally sure knowledge that Scripture enjoins me to care for my body. Does this mean that I think about Jesus with every jumping jack? Not at all. What it means is that my exercising is not merely a capitulation to a fitness-crazy culture, but rather is an attempt at obedience. God created this body of mine; the least I can do is try halfheartedly to take care of it.[1]

Where do you need support and encouragement in your prayer life? Would a prayer partner be helpful? Think of someone whose spirit you trust and respect, and consider if you are willing to ask that person to be your partner. Sometimes we hesitate to seek such a relationship for fear of intruding, presuming intimacy, or getting no for an answer. Remember that asking others to become prayer partners indicates that you hold them in high regard. Your invitation to pray with and for them could be experienced as a gift, even if they must refuse.

Praying for Others

Beyond the mutual support of prayer partners, we are asked to pray for others in our church communities—often people we do not know well. After naming people in need of prayer in weekly worship, pastors may encourage their congregations to pray for these people during the week. Other times we may be asked individually to offer prayers for another. "People often ask me to pray," a woman told me. "Someone will call and ask for prayers for a son or mother or some other situation. I always say yes. I can't imagine saying no. But then I hang up the phone and am not sure what to do." Have you ever felt that way?

Some intercessory prayers take the form of specific requests such as when asking God for healing in another's life or for reconciliation within a family or community. Other intercessory prayers ask God to grant the person in trouble courage, patience, or hope. Some simply say, "God, be with her. Christ, be present to him." At an intercessory prayer retreat a man shared the way he prayed: "I often have no idea of what a person needs," he said. "So I imagine the person surrounded by the light of the Trinity. I hold him or her within a glowing triangle, gazing with my heart until the image fades and another person arises to be prayed for."

> ***Intercessory prayer means discovering that we do not have to do it all nor do it all alone.***
> **—Ann and Barry Ulanov**

Because of so many requests for prayer, churches often organize prayer chains or establish intercessory prayer ministries. I have found the latter to be more consistent and powerful within congregations, because a prayer chain is likely to turn into a telephone tree. A telephone tree or any other organized way of sharing information within a community is helpful when all members need to know of a sudden death, the birth of a child, or the cancellation of a worship service due to snow. Some faithful folks in the chain may pray for the concerns communicated, but a depth commitment to prayer cannot always be assumed.

One church, in order to become more intentional about praying for others, organized an intercessory prayer team in the following manner. A request went out to the whole church for people to serve the congregation in this way. Those who volunteered met with the pastor to be educated about the practice of intercessory prayer and to discuss questions and concerns about their role in the life of the church. They made a pledge of confidentiality and were asked to commit to the ministry for one year.

The congregation was then asked to relay prayer requests to the pastor or lay leader who then notified members of the prayer team. Those requesting prayer could tell as much or as little about their situation as they wished. One person might ask for prayers that a spouse be offered a specific job. Another might simply say, "My family is having a hard time right now. We need prayers." Others might share their struggles in depth with the pastor but request that the prayer team know only the outline of their concerns.

A member of this prayer ministry reflected on how privileged she felt to be part of other people's lives through prayer. "I set aside a time every morning to pray for the people who have been entrusted to me," she said. "I use both words and images. I hold my hands cupped in front of my heart, imagining that I am holding the problems and concerns as well as the possibility of wholeness and healing for each person. After a time of silent prayer I lift my hands slowly upward, then open them to indicate my desire to turn this situation over to God. I pray this way for each person. I have discovered that I do not need to know any details of their concerns to pray for others and grow closer to them in my heart."

Sometimes prayer needs words, but not so many, and not so many times repeated.
—Kristen Ingram Johnson

This prayer ministry allowed members of the congregation to request prayer without sharing details. Their privacy was honored, yet they received the support of the church through prayer. Many people told the pastor how comforting it was to know they were being prayed for. They recognized the blessing of being part of a praying congregation.

We began this week thinking about the Christian call to community and the value of praying with and for others particularly in weekly worship. I mentioned the common liturgical prayers we share and the joy we can find in speaking and listening with others to the prayers of our tradition. I began seminary planning to pursue a solitary spiritual journey. I have since discovered that praying with and for others is essential if I am to grow in faith and discipleship. This became clear to me a few years ago after a long illness. When I finally had the strength to leave the house, the first place I wanted to go was to church. As my husband helped me walk into the sanctuary for a Sunday service, I began to weep. I knew I had come home. Hearing the music, seeing love and compassion on the faces of the community that had been praying for me, I was sure I no longer wanted to be a Christian alone.

DAILY EXERCISES

This week you are reminded that in practicing the Christian life your prayers in community are of central importance. Read Week 9, "Praying with and for Others." Keep your journal at hand so you can record feelings, insights, memories, and questions that arise as you read the article and complete each exercise. Stay attuned to where the Spirit prompts you to pray with or for others this week.

EXERCISE 1 BEING COMMUNITY

Read Acts 2:42-47; 4:32-37; 5:1-6. These stories from the early church reflect both the glory and the fall of Christian community, its ability and inability to live its prayer and be faithful to God's dream. Reflect on what it means to be a faithful community of Christians. Record your ideas in your journal.

Now turn your thoughts to your own life and experiences. What faith communities have you belonged to? List them, remembering also those that may be closest at hand—for example, your family, a circle of friends, and other small faith groups. What have been the enduring gifts of those experiences? In what ways have you experienced the glory and the failure of Christian community?

Pray for your communities of faith, past and present. Place your spiritual journey and the journeys of these communities in God's hands and give thanks.

EXERCISE 2 PRAYING TOGETHER

Read the "The Prayer of Saint Francis" (page 117). Corporate prayer is a long held tradition for Christians and Jews. Something wonderful and mysterious happens when our voices unite as one. The prayers themselves can take on new dimensions when they are raised up together. "The Prayer of Saint Francis" will serve as our example. These inspiring words have been sung and prayed by Christians since the thirteenth century.

Prepare your sacred space and assume a prayerful posture. Offer the prayer as your own, praying slowly and deliberately, picturing in your mind situations where you can be an instrument of God's peace. What kind of difference can God make through you? Express your gratitude.

Now, as you read the prayer again, think of a faith group you are part of. As you pray, change *me* to *us* and *I* to *we*. Picture situations where your group can be an instrument of God's peace together. What difference can God make through you?

In your journal, write about your experience of private and corporate prayer. What insights have you gained?

Exercise 3 Interceding for One Another

Read Mark 10:13-16. Another form of praying together in community is intercession on one another's behalf. One way to intercede in love is to imagine yourself, like the people who brought children to Jesus "in order that he might touch them," bringing your children or your companions or other members of your faith community to be touched and held in the loving arms of Jesus. (You might read the words of the old hymn, "Leaning on the Everlasting Arms" to inspire your visualization.)

Assume a comfortable prayer posture and begin, in your mind's eye, to escort one person at a time to Jesus. Watch as Jesus embraces each one in turn. When you have completed your visualizations of others, approach Jesus yourself to be touched and blessed. Feel the divine arms closing around you. Let the love fill your heart and soul. Now imagine all of your companions joining you. You are all held in the arms of Jesus. Offer words of praise and thanksgiving. Spend a few minutes journaling your thoughts and feelings.

Exercise 4 Considering Your Community

Read Acts 2:42-47. The early Christians "devoted themselves to the apostles' teaching and fellowship, to the breaking of bread and the prayers." What do you imagine characterized the prayer life of that early Christian community? Record your thoughts.

Now think about your *Companions in Christ* community. What do you appreciate most about the prayer life of your group? What is the quality of trust, intimacy, or willingness to risk that has developed? How have certain styles of prayer seemed more helpful than others for the community? Note thoughts in your journal.

Write your prayer for your *Companions* community. Pray by heart the prayer you've written.

Exercise 5 Writing a Prayer

Read your journal notes from the last exercise. This is your chance to plan a way to pray with your *Companions* group in order to enhance your corporate prayer life. Follow a model that the group has used before or experiment with something new. If praying out loud makes you nervous, consider these possibilities: write out every word, plan a time of silent prayer, consider a body prayer or a musical prayer, or find a printed prayer that inspires you and make copies for everyone. Remember, the goal is to enhance your group's prayer life together. The leader will invite you to share your prayer at some point during this week's session.

In your journal write down your plans and what you hope will happen, including any materials or equipment you might need (for example, a CD player for musical prayer). Offer your plans and preparations to God for blessing.

Remember to review your journal entries for the week in preparation for the group meeting.

The Prayer of Saint Francis

Lord, make me an instrument of thy peace;
where there is hatred, let me sow love;
where there is injury, pardon; where there is doubt, faith;
where there is despair, hope;
where there is darkness, light;
and where there is sadness, joy.

O Divine Master,
grant that I may not so much seek
to be consoled as to console;
to be understood, as to understand;
to be loved, as to love;
for it is in giving that we receive,
it is in pardoning that we are pardoned,
and it is in dying that we are born to eternal life.

Week 10

Prayer and Social Transformation

Hundreds of people from all walks of life gathered on the steps of the Colorado State Capitol on August 6, 2005. We were joining our hearts and voices in prayer on the sixtieth anniversary of the bombing of Hiroshima. We came together to mourn those killed and wounded in the attack and to ask forgiveness for our part in the tragedy of war. After hearing from a Japanese man who had been in Hiroshima that fateful day, we walked silently, carrying candles, to a nearby church for a service of repentance and hope. We listened to scripture, prayed silently, and lifted our voices in song. I left the prayer service with a feeling of deep grief intertwined with profound hope. Maybe together, with God's help, our prayers and actions could prevent another nuclear tragedy.

This time of prayer held such power and possibility because we were praying not only for social transformation but for God's saving grace in our own hearts. Howard Thurman, twentieth-century African American theologian and mystic, wrote, "You can't stand in the midst of the world and struggle for fundamental change unless you are standing in your own space and looking for change within."[1] The leaders of our small gathering guided us in prayers for our own transformation as well as for changes in the world. Praying for forgiveness was as important as praying for the realization of God's promise of justice and peace. Our prayers of confession mingled with prayers for strength and courage to "do justice, and to love kindness, and to walk humbly with [our] God" (Mic. 6:8). We were praying for ourselves as well as for others.

Our prayer makes a difference in who we are and what we become.
—Margaret Guenther

Intercessory Prayer

Last week we discussed the power of praying with and for one another in our worshiping communities. Now we are challenged to take our prayers beyond our families, friends, and congregations to the wider world. This opportunity raises interesting questions, as I discovered in a discussion about prayer and social justice when a woman shared the following concern: "I know how to pray for the people I love, and even those I do not know well," she said. "But how do I pray for unknown victims of an earthquake or for all the hungry people of the world? The suffering is so pervasive I don't know what to say." I'm sure that we all have felt this way at times.

When I am not sure what to say in my prayers for the world, an image from Quaker philosopher Douglas Steere is helpful. He writes that when we pray for others—individuals or situations in need of healing and transformation—the words of our prayers are not intended to provide God with a solution to the problem, nor do our longings bring God to those people or places. God knows what is needed and is already there. Our prayers simply and profoundly serve to "lower the threshold in the person [or situation] prayed for and to make the besieging love of God . . . slightly more visible and more inviting."[2] He uses *threshold* as an image of our internal resistance to God's ever-present love.

Steere goes on to say that prayers of intercession also serve to lower the threshold of the one who is praying. Therefore, when I pray for people who are refugees, not only do they become more available to God's "besieging love," but so do I. By praying for others I make myself vulnerable, and with God's grace I may see the need for transformation in my own heart. I might recognize a lack of compassion in the way I treat others or become aware of ways I misuse power. I may discover seeds of violence in my own heart and the need to pray for personal healing. With my threshold of self-defense lowered, I might come to see the situation I am praying for more clearly and recognize some action to take—a small step toward justice and peace.

There is no form of prayer that is more obviously an act of real love than the costly act of intercessory prayer.
—Douglas V. Steere

A woman praying daily for peace in the Middle East and an end to the cycle of violence began to sense fear at the heart of that conflict. Her insight led her to ask where her own fear kept her trapped in discord. Her estrangement from her beloved daughter came instantly to mind. She was startled to realize that fear, her own and most likely her daughter's, was at the center of their conflict. She decided to stop allowing fear to rule her behavior and reached out in love to her daughter. "I cannot do much to resolve the conflicts in the world," she told her prayer group, "but there are things I can do to facilitate healing within my own family." In doing so, she probably realized that every healing, however small, contributes to the healing of the whole world.

As we envision intercessory prayer lowering thresholds of resistance in ourselves and others, our words become less important than our longing for healing and wholeness throughout the world. We do not have to decide what words to utter or wonder whether we are praying correctly. We can simply focus our attention on the area of concern and pray whatever is in our hearts.

The Longing of Our Hearts

Bill, the ten-year-old hero of Mary Ellis's recent novel *The Turtle Warrior*, let his heart guide him in praying for his older brother who had left home to fight in the Vietnam War. Bill went to the Catholic Church with his mother and knelt in front of a bank of candles. Taking a taper, Bill lit every votive candle before him. Then he assumed a posture of prayer with eyes tightly shut and called his brother to mind.

> He tried to think of a prayer. But the formal prayers of the church didn't mean anything to him. Then it came to him. He whispered the only thing he could think to say. "Come home, come home, come home, come home."[3]

Bill had been taught prayers at home and in church, but none of them felt right for his intense experience of loss, fear, and hope. This did not, however, keep him from praying. He found a way to honor his brother's parting words: "Pray for me." We can follow Bill's example when we are faced with situations for which all the ways we have been taught to pray do not seem adequate. We listen to our hearts and start there.

Perhaps we simply begin with these words: "O God, I do not know how to pray in the face of such evil." We might call out, "Help me to pray, Lord, help me to pray!" Sometimes we think we know what God should do in a given situation, and we begin with our best ideas: "God of justice, where are you? Soften the hearts of those abusing powers. Fill their hearts with compassion. Now! Please, before more damage is done." At other times we may be so caught up in our own personal despair that we cannot see the needs of the world. Then we plead for courage, hope, or healing in our own lives, trusting that when we are ready the Holy One will expand them into prayers for the world.

Prayer practice is the art of setting aside our own individual desires to seek the desire that God has placed on our heart.
—Daniel Wolpert

Trying to figure out how to pray before we begin leaves the transforming grace of God out of the process. Beginning to pray where our hearts actually are connects us to that holy relationship within which our thresholds of resistance are lowered and divine love gradually guides us into transformed prayers and hearts. A man shared the truth of this spiritual dynamic in his own life when he spoke of his month-long experience of praying for victims of domestic violence:

> I began my prayers by telling God to give the victims what I thought they needed—the courage to leave their abusive situations. I continued to pray for their courage during the first week but gradually began to feel more compassion for their situations, recognizing their terror and helplessness. My prayer began to soften; I became less demanding. I began to beg God to let the victims know they were loved and not alone in their struggles. I continued to pray in this way for many more days until I was astounded to find myself praying for the perpetrators. Through prayer my heart had opened so I could begin to see how wounded these cruel people must be. I saw them trapped in a cycle of violence of their own making, finding no way to escape. My prayer shifted again, this time for healing and wholeness for victims and perpetrators alike. As I prayed this way for many more days, I realized that my heart as well as my prayers had been transformed. I had discovered compassion for those I had thought to be my enemies.

Praying for Enemies

"Love your enemies and pray for those who persecute you," Jesus said (Matt. 5:44). But like the man's experience in the story above, I have discovered that I must first pray for those who persecute me (and others I experience as enemies) if I am ever to learn to love them. If I try to love my enemies on my own, before turning to God in prayer, I will never pray for them. I need God's help to grow into this difficult love.

If we are honest with ourselves and God, our first prayers for our enemies will likely be filled with anger and hurt. We may shout and cry about what has been done to us or our loved ones. We may rage against groups and nations that persecute others, ignore the plight of the poor and ill, and do nothing to end conflict and war. When these difficult feelings fill our hearts, we can turn to the Psalms for guidance, for the Hebrew people knew how to cry out to God against their enemies:

> O my God, make them like whirling dust,
> like chaff before the wind.
> As fire consumes the forest,
> as the flame sets the mountains ablaze,
> so pursue them with your tempest
> and terrify them with your hurricane.
> Fill their faces with shame,
> so that they may seek your name, O LORD.
> Let them be put to shame and dismayed forever;
> let them perish in disgrace. (Psalm 83:13-17)

Praying our rage, grief, frustration, and desire for revenge brings us into relationship with God who hears our anger and pain. But God will not leave us there, for our prayers and our hearts will slowly be transformed. I discovered this years ago when I lived in northern California, and a trailside killer roamed the surrounding hills. I prayed my sorrow about those who had been killed. I cried out to God my fear and anger, as well as the frustration I felt at being barred from the trails I loved. I was unsparing in the things I wanted God to do to this evil person.

One Sunday morning during worship, as I silently continued my raging prayers to God about this stranger, I felt a sudden shift, a softening of my heart. I began to recognize the broken spirit, the pain, and fear of this unknown enemy. I imagined his alienation, his fear, and his compulsion to kill. With my heart opened by God's grace I found myself praying, "O, my God, help him, help him. O, my God, help him."

It may be that we have only rage to offer God, and it will seem that there is only silence in response. But the prayer has to be prayed. The alternative is a far more serious death—the death of relationship with God.

—Elizabeth J. Canham

God Responds

When we pray for social transformation in whatever way we can, we may feel God's grace in our hearts and experience changes in our prayers and behaviors. But we rarely see answers or resolutions to the problems about which we pray. People worldwide are still hungry and homeless. Wars, violence, and oppression continue. To pray fervently and see no results is discouraging, tempting us to quit our prayers. But we must continue even in the face of despair. When we pray for nothing less than to see the reign of God become a reality, we do not say our prayers a few times and then let them go. As John Calvin wrote, "We must repeat the same supplications not twice or three times only, but as often as we have need, a hundred and a thousand times. . . . We must never be weary in waiting for God's help."[4]

What does God's help look like? How are we expecting God to respond to our fervent supplications? I believe we often get discouraged when we don't see a miraculous intervention in response to our prayers. The Bible is full of vivid stories of God's miracles. We may have had our own experiences of divine intervention. But lack of a visible intervention in the world's problems does not signal God's refusal to answer our prayers, for the Holy Mystery has other ways of responding.

Rather than intervening, God often interacts with humankind, helping us take steps to make the changes we long for. Rather than bringing divine power from on high, the Spirit empowers us to act in the world for reconciliation and healing. The story of the woman who reached out to her daughter in love exemplifies divine interaction. Her prayers helped her see her own fear and guided her to new behavior. We also witness divine interaction that transforms our world when strangers find welcome in our communities, when people work together to improve education for all children, and when people volunteer to go to war-torn countries with much needed medical supplies.

What if this divine interaction still does not result in the desired outcome? Is that a sign that God has abandoned us, and we are alone? We can learn of another way God responds to our prayers from the story of a man whose young daughter was ill with cancer. Many people prayed for her, but God did not intervene to cure her. Others were experiencing the wonder of divine interaction as physicians, nurses, family, and friends provided medical expertise and loving care. Still, the child continued to lose strength and ultimately died.

When asked by a friend how he could believe in God after this tragedy, the father replied that although God had not intervened to cure her and God's interaction with her care team had been unable to save her, he had known God's presence because both he and his daughter had been able to endure the suffering caused by her illness. Now with her death, he was able to endure his grief. The child's father believed that God was responding to prayer by being present in the midst of suffering, offering comfort, consolation, and strength.

Such a story may help us persevere in prayer for social transformation even when we see no results. We can trust God is with us when we are praying and present to those for whom we offer prayers. God's besieging love may not change the situation in any visible way, but those of us involved are granted the courage and grace to endure as we continue to pray and act in ways that make possible the creation of a new heaven and a new earth. After all, we never know when our prayers may help to lower all the thresholds of resistance in a complex social situation or when God may use our prayers to usher in some great divine purpose.

> ***In prayer, nothing is ever wasted.***
> **—Roberta C. Bondi**

Creating the Future

"History belongs to intercessors who believe the future into being," writes theologian and peace activist Walter Wink. He goes on to say that intercessory prayer, "far from being an escape from action, is a means of focusing for action and of creating action."[5] Remember our understanding that anything we do to honor, deepen, or strengthen our relationship with God can be called prayer? With this intention in place, the actions that grow from intercessory prayer can themselves become prayers.

When we stand with others at a prayer vigil for peace or mentor prisoners in gaining life skills, we are praying. Speaking out against prejudice and oppression, teaching children alternatives to violence, and writing prophetic poetry can all be forms of prayer. Knitting prayer blankets for the elderly, cooking at the soup kitchen, and building Habitat for Humanity homes can become our prayers for social transformation. Standing up for justice, raising our voices to promote peace, using our hands to bring comfort and solace are all opportunities to become as

> ***It has always been the Christian view that every bit of work done toward God is a prayer.***
> **—Evelyn Underhill**

Christ in this troubled world. Teresa of Ávila understood this centuries ago when she wrote:

> Christ has no body now on earth but yours, no hands but yours, no feet but yours. Yours are the eyes through which Christ's compassion is to look out to the world. Yours are the feet with which Christ is to go about doing good. Yours are the hands with which Christ is to bless all people now.[6]

Reflecting on Our Experience

As your ten-week exploration of the way of prayer draws to a close it will be wise to reflect on your experience, asking how you might continue to engage in prayer now that the study is complete. Explore how your understanding of prayer has grown during your reading, reflections, practices, and group discussions. Looking back over the various prayer forms you have experienced, consider the methods you enjoyed, the ones you found difficult, and those you feel called to include in your ongoing prayer life.

After this reflection, allow plans for your personal way of prayer to begin to take form in your mind and heart. Be realistic as you discover the shape of your prayer life, and be gentle with yourself as you begin to practice. Be willing to experiment so you can find the ways of prayer that best suit you. Remember that you are not doing this on your own. God will guide, comfort, and encourage you in the process, for the Holy One is calling you to a relationship of eternal love.

DAILY EXERCISES

In this final week you are invited to plumb the relationship between prayer and change, both personally and in the larger world. As you yearn for the healing of divisions and conflict, there are perspectives here to help shape your prayers. Read Week 10, "Prayer and Social Transformation." Use your journal to capture insights, hopes, prayers, and questions as you read the article and respond to each daily exercise. Note ways in which these themes connect with earlier weeks.

EXERCISE 1 PRAYING THE FAMILIAR

Read Matthew 6:9-13. The Lord's Prayer is familiar to most Christians though we often associate it with ritual prayer. Explore the intercessory nature of the Lord's Prayer by recording the words of the prayer in your journal, writing each phrase on a separate line. Go through the phrases one at a time and identify a prayer for social transformation related to or implied in each. What are we asking God to do in and for the world? What are we offering to do in and for the world? When you finish journaling, intercede for the world by praying the prayer the Lord taught us.

EXERCISE 2 PRAYING THE NEED

Read John 3:16. If you have access to a globe or world atlas, in print or online, spend some time with it. Look carefully at the seven continents and the names of the various countries. Gaze at them lovingly. Hear the words of John 3:16: "For God so loved the world. . . ." On the globe or map, gently trace lands and borders with your fingers. Call to mind areas where you are aware of a need for social transformation. Let your eyes and fingers come to rest in one place. Focus on the need you recognize there. Consider it prayerfully. In God's presence ask yourself what may be at the heart of the situation that requires transformation.

Offer the region and the need to God in prayer. Then reflect on your experience in your journal. What has your prayer for others taught you about yourself?

EXERCISE 3 PRAYING THE DIFFICULT

Read Romans 8:18-27. Paul tells us that "the whole creation" and "we ourselves" are "groaning in labor pains" in the process of waiting for rebirth as a new creation through Christ. As you read these verses, get in touch with the places of suffering and groaning in society or in your relationships where you experience the greatest difficulty praying for change. Choose one such place.

Prepare yourself for prayer concerning that place. Remember the assurance of the same passage of scripture: "Likewise the Spirit helps us in our weakness; for we do not know how to pray as we ought, but that very Spirit intercedes with sighs too deep for words" (v. 26).

Lift up the concern with or without words. Ask the Spirit to intercede in your prayer, for the Spirit to pray in and through you. Entrust the people and the circumstances into God's loving care. Remain silent in God's presence until you sense that your prayer is complete. In your journal, record your reflections.

Exercise 4 Praying with Persistence

Read Luke 18:1-8. Prayers for social transformation often require great patience. Immediately discernible results are rare. Waves of change often occur slowly. Jesus invites us to be as persistent in our prayers for the reign of God on earth, as was the widow seeking justice. Read the parable again and identify with the widow. Where are you tempted to lose heart and give up on seeking positive social change? Put your thoughts on paper.

Take heart from Jesus' parable that we should not give up in prayer. Approach God concerning a situation that seems closed to change. Clearly name the need and obstacles. If you're feeling frustrated or impatient, say so. If the problem seems overwhelming, admit it. If you can see a solution, acknowledge it. Persist in your intercession.

When you have finished, become quiet; wait and listen. Reflect in your journal on where you sense God is in relation to your prayer concern. Do you feel you have to "talk God into caring," that you are yielding to God's persistent care, or that you are becoming a partner in God's work? Record your sense of what God is calling you to do next in persistent prayer and action.

Exercise 5 Praying the Way

Read Colossians 1:9-12. Paul prays regularly for the new creation to come about within his companions in Christ. Social transformation can begin with God's grace at work in one heart at a time. As you read these verses, lift your *Companions* group in prayer. Consider which of these verses inspire your prayer for the group or for individuals in the group. Then let those verses carry you into a time of prayer for each group member.

You and your companions have devoted ten weeks to this study of *The Way of Prayer*. Reflect on these questions in your journal: How do you perceive the grace of God at work in your midst? Where do you see more room for growth? What do you desire for yourself and for your companions as you continue your spiritual journeys? Make some notes on your insights about these three questions that you would like to share with your group at your final session for this study.

Close with the prayer from Psalm 19:14: "Let the words of my mouth and the meditation of my heart be acceptable to you, O Lord, my rock and my redeemer."

Remember to review your journal entries for the week in preparation for the group meeting.

Notes

Week 1: How Do You Pray?

1. Ann Ulanov and Barry Ulanov, *Primary Speech: A Psychology of Prayer* (Atlanta, Ga.: John Knox Press, 1982), 2.
2. Sam Keen, *Hymns to an Unknown God: Awakening the Spirit in Everyday Life* (New York: Bantam Books, 1994), 71.
3. "All Creatures of Our God and King," lyrics by Francis of Assisi, trans. William H. Draper, *United Methodist Hymnal* (Nashville, Tenn.: United Methodist Publishing House, 1989), no. 62.

Week 2: Images of God

1. Dietrich Bonhoeffer, *Letters and Papers from Prison*, enlarged edition, ed. Eberhard Bethge (New York: Macmillan Publishing Co., 1972), 282.
2. Thomas Merton, audiotape, 1965, given to Marcus J. Borg by Reverend David McConnell, pastor of the United Methodist Church in Lewistown, Montana, and quoted in Marcus J. Borg, *The God We Never Knew: Beyond Dogmatic Religion to a More Authentic Contemporary Faith* (San Francisco: HarperSanFrancisco, 1997), 47.
3. Borg, *The God We Never Knew,* 32.
4. Marjorie Hewitt Suchocki, *In God's Presence: Theological Reflections on Prayer* (St. Louis, Mo.: Chalice Press, 1996), 12.
5. Roberta C. Bondi, *In Ordinary Time: Healing the Wounds of the Heart* (Nashville, Tenn.: Abingdon Press, 1996), 22–23.

Week 3: Praying by Heart

1. Thomas H. Troeger, *Above the Moon Earth Rises: Hymn Texts, Anthems and Poems for a New Creation* (New York: Oxford University Press, 2002).
2. Keith Beasley-Topliffe, "Jesus Prayer," in *The Upper Room Dictionary of Christian Spiritual Formation*, ed. Keith Beasley-Topliffe (Nashville, Tenn.: Upper Room Books, 2003), 151.
3. *The Way of a Pilgrim*, fwd. Walter J. Ciszek, trans. Helen Bacovcin (New York: Image Books, 1978).

4. See Jane E. Vennard, "The Way of a Pilgrim," in *Dictionary of Christian Spiritual Formation*, 287.
5. Richard J. Foster, *Prayer: Finding the Heart's True Home* (San Francisco: HarperSanFrancisco, 1992), 136.
6. Adapted from Ron DelBene, Herb Montgomery, and Mary Montgomery, *The Breath of Life: A Workbook* (Nashville, Tenn.: Upper Room Books, 1996), 12–13. Used by permission of Upper Room Books.
7. Mary Margaret Funk, *Tools Matter for Practicing the Spiritual Life* (New York: Continuum, 2001), 96.

Week 4: Praying with Music

1. *Hildegard of Bingen's Book of Divine Works with Letters and Songs*, ed. Matthew Fox (Santa Fe, N.M.: Bear and Company, 1987), 358.
2. Fanny Crosby, cited in D. Darrell Woomer, "Hymns," *Dictionary of Christian Spiritual Formation*, 138.
3. Woomer, "Hymns," in *Dictionary of Christian Spiritual Formation*, 139.
4. Ibid.
5. Brother Roger, "Preparing for a Time of Prayer," *Songs and Prayers from Taizé* (Chicago: GIA Publications, 1991), 5.
6. David Steindl-Rast with Sharon Lebell, *The Music of Silence: Entering the Sacred Space of Monastic Experience* (New York: HarperCollins/HarperSanFrancisco, 1995), 20.
7. James A. Laurie, "One Love," *Flobots Present . . . Platypus*, CD, 2005). www.flobots.com.
8. Jane Redmont, *When in Doubt, Sing: Prayer in Daily Life* (New York: HarperCollinsPublishers, 1999), 312.
9. Terry Tempest Williams, *Refuge: An Unnatural History of Family and Place* (New York: Vintage Books, 1991), 149.
10. Gary Zukav, *Soul Stories* (New York: Simon & Schuster, 2000), 117.

Week 5: Praying by Gaze

1. Thomas Merton, *A Search for Solitude: Pursuing the Monk's True Life*, ed. Lawrence S. Cunningham (San Francisco: HarperSanFrancisco, 1996), 181–82.
2. Ibid., 182–83.
3. Meister Eckhart, cited in Jan Phillips, *Divining the Body: Reclaim the Holiness of Your Physical Self* (Woodstock, Vt.: SkyLight Paths Publishing, 2005), 186.

Week 6: Praying with Our Bodies

1. Jane E. Vennard, *Praying with Body and Soul: A Way to Intimacy with God* (Minneapolis, Minn.: Augsburg Fortress Publishers, 1998).
2. *The Collected Works of St. John of the Cross*, trans. Kieran Kavanaugh and Otilio Rodriguez (Washington, D.C.: ICS Publications, 1973), 413.

3. Sonny Brewer, *The Poet of Tolstoy Park* (New York: Ballantine Books, 2005), 128.
4. Ibid., 227.
5. Wendy M. Wright, "Lawrence of the Resurrection," *Dictionary of Christian Spiritual Formation*, 167.
6. Douglas V. Steere, *Dimensions of Prayer: Cultivating a Relationship with God*, rev. ed. (Nashville, Tenn.: Upper Room Books, 1997), 15.
7. Barbara Brown Taylor, "Practicing Incarnation," *Christian Century* 122, no. 7 (April 5, 2005): 39.
8. Philip Simmons, *Learning to Fall: The Blessings of an Imperfect Life* (New York: Bantam Books, 2003), 37.
9. David Scott, "Mother Teresa's Hunger for God," *St. Anthony Messenger*, Web site, http://www.American Catholic.org/Messenger/Sep 2005/feature2.asp

Week 7: Scriptural Prayer

1. Chester P. Michael and Marie C. Norrisey, *Prayer and Temperament: Different Prayer Forms for Different Personality Types* (Charlottesville, Va.: The Open Door, 1984), 32.
2. Saint Ignatius of Loyola, trans. Louis J. Puhl, *The Spiritual Exercises of St. Ignatius* (Chicago: Loyola University Press, 1951).
3. Katherine Dyckman, Mary Garvin, and Elizabeth Liebert, *The Spiritual Exercises Reclaimed: Uncovering Liberating Possibilities for Women* (New York: Paulist Press, 2001), ix.
4. Ignatius, *Spiritual Exercises*, 25.
5. Patricia D. Brown, "Examen," in *Dictionary of Christian Spiritual Formation*, 99. See also "The Prayer of Examen," in Richard J. Foster's *Prayer: Finding the Heart's True Home.*
6. Ibid., 99–100.

Week 8: Contemplative Prayer

1. "Journal," in Albert C. Outler, ed., John Wesley, in *A Library of Protestant Thought* (New York: Oxford University Press, 1964), 66.
2. Thomas Merton, *Contemplative Prayer* (New York: Herder and Herder, 1969), 115.
3. Avery Brooke, "What Is Contemplation? A Kaleidoscope of Answers," *Weavings* 7, no. 4 (July/Aug 1992): 10.
4. Kent Ira Groff, "Negative Way," in *Dictionary of Christian Spiritual Formation*, 198.
5. *The Cloud of Unknowing*, trans. Ira Progoff (New York: Dell Publishing, 1957), 61.
6. Thomas Keating, *Invitation to Love: The Way of Christian Contemplation* (Rockport, Mass.: Element, 1992), 90.
7. There are discernment methods in the Ignatian tradition and recent adaptations of that tradition, such as Danny E. Morris and Charles M. Olsen, *Discerning God's Will Together: A Spiritual Practice for the Church* (Nashville, Tenn.: Upper Room Books,

1997). These methods do not guarantee a true discernment but can prepare us to receive the gift of discernment.

8. Wendy M. Wright, "Passing Angels: The Arts of Spiritual Discernment," *Weavings* 10, no. 6 (Nov/Dec 1995): 12.

Week 9: Praying with and for Others

1. Lauren F. Winner, *Mudhouse Sabbath* (Brewster, Mass.: Paraclete Press, 2003), 76-77.

Week 10: Prayer and Social Transformation

1. Howard Thurman, cited in Marjorie Colton, ed., *Spirit Unfolding: The Newsletter of the Spiritual Development Network of the United Church of Christ*, (Winter 1997): 1.
2. Douglas V. Steere, "Intercession: Caring for Souls," *Weavings* 4, no. 2 (Mar/Apr 1989): 19-20.
3. Mary Relindes Ellis, *The Turtle Warrior* (New York: Viking, 2004), 53.
4. John Calvin, *Sermons on the Epistle to the Ephesians* (Carlisle, Pa.: Banner of Truth Trust, 1973), 683.
5. Walter Wink, *The Powers That Be: Theology for a New Millennium* (New York: Doubleday, 1998); 185, 187.
6. Prayer attributed to Teresa of Ávila, sixteenth-century mystic.

Sources and Authors of Margin Quotes

Week 1 How Do You Pray?

Timothy Jones, *The Art of Prayer* (New York: Ballantine Books, 1997), 8.

Thomas Merton, in M. Basil Pennington, *Centering Prayer* (New York: Image Books, 1982), 56.

W. Paul Jones, "Prayer as Living Itself," *Weavings* (May/June 1998): 32.

Daniel Wolpert, *Creating a Life with God: The Call of Ancient Prayer Practices* (Nashville, Tenn.: Upper Room Books, 2003), 29.

Richard Rohr, *Everything Belongs: The Gift of Contemplative Prayer* (New York: Crossroad, 1989), 29.

Mark Yaconelli and Alexx Campbell, "Prayer," in *Way to Live: Christian Practices for Teens*, ed. Dorothy C. Bass and Don C. Richter (Nashville, Tenn.: Upper Room Books, 2002), 278.

Dom John Chapman, cited in Thelma Hall, *Too Deep for Words: Rediscovering Lectio Divina* (New York: Paulist Press, 1988), 40.

Week 2 Images of God

John S. Mogabgab, "Editor's Introduction," *Weavings* (Mar/Apr 1989): 2.

Roberta C. Bondi, "The Paradox of Prayer," *Weavings* (Mar/Apr 1989): 8.

James Emery White, *The Prayer God Longs For* (Downers Grove, Ill.: InterVarsity Press, 2005), 23.

Ibid., 17.

Douglas V. Steere, *Dimensions of Prayer: Cultivating a Relationship with God*, rev. ed. (Nashville, Tenn.: Upper Room Books, 1997), 48–49.

Isaac of Syria, "Directions on Spiritual Training" in eds., E. Kadloubovsky and G.E.H. Palmer, *Early Fathers from the Philokalia* (London: Faber and Faber, 1954), 206.

Week 3 Praying by Heart

Irma Zaleski, *Living the Jesus Prayer* (New York: Continuum, 1998), 4.

Wendy M. Wright, "Seasons of Glad Songs: Entries from a Notebook on Scripture and Prayer," *Weavings* (Jul/Aug 1996): 14.

Roberta C. Bondi, "The Paradox of Prayer," *Weavings* (Mar/Apr 1989): 9.

Thomas Keating, "Cultivating the Centering Prayer," in Thomas Keating, M. Basil Pennington, and Thomas I. Clarke, *Finding Grace at the Center* (Petersham, Mass.: St. Bede's Publications, 1978), 30.

Thomas Kelly, *A Testament of Devotion* (San Francisco: HarperSanFrancisco, 1996) 35.

Richard Baxter, *The Saints' Everlasting Rest* (Glasgow: William Collins, 1844), 314.

WEEK 4 PRAYING WITH MUSIC

Avery Brooke, *Hidden in Plain Sight: The Practice of Christian Meditation* (Nashville, Tenn.: Abingdon Press, 1986), 94.

Ibid., 89.

Ibid., 81.

Ibid., 93.

WEEK 5 PRAYING BY GAZE

Carlo Carretto, *The God Who Comes*, cited in Rueben P. Job and Norman Shawchuck, *A Guide to Prayer for Ministers and Other Servants* (Nashville, Tenn.: Upper Room Books, 1983), 15.

Nouwen, *Behold the Beauty of the Lord: Praying with Icons* (Notre Dame, Ind.: Ave Maria Press, 1987), 14.

Yaconelli and Campbell, "Prayer," in *Way to Live*, 282.

Nouwen, *Behold the Beauty of the Lord,*, 95.

Henri J. M. Nouwen, *The Wounded Healer: Ministry in Contemporary Society*, cited in Job and Shawchuck, *A Guide to Prayer*, 23.

Saint Francis of Assisi, cited in Jan Phillips, *Divining the Body: Reclaim the Holiness of Your Physical Self* (Woodstock, Vt.: Skylight Path Publishing, 2005), 191.

WEEK 6 PRAYING WITH OUR BODIES

Wolpert, *Creating a Life with God*, 116.

Ibid., 120.

Ibid., 123.

Gunilla Norris, *Being Home: Discovering the Spiritual in the Everyday* (Mahwah, N.J.: Hidden Spring, 2001), 13.

E. Glenn Hinson, "Praying without Ceasing," *Weavings* (May/June 1998): 36.

Frederick Buechner, *Now and Then* (San Francisco: Harper & Row, 1983), 87.

Barbara Brown Taylor, "Practicing Incarnation," *The Christian Century* (April 5, 2005): 39.

WEEK 7 SCRIPTURAL PRAYER

Elizabeth J. Canham, *Heart Whispers: Benedictine Wisdom for Today* (Nashville, Tenn.: Upper Room Books, 1999), 25.

Virginia Ramey Mollenkott, *Speech, Silence, Action!* cited in Job and Shawchuck, *A Guide to Prayer*, 103.

Dietrich Bonhoeffer, *Meditating on the Word*, ed. David McI. Gracie (Nashville, Tenn.: Upper Room, 1986), 44.

Richard Foster, *Celebration of Discipline* (San Francisco: HarperSanFrancisco, 1998), 25.

Ibid., 30.

Calvin: Institutes of the Christian Religion, ed. John T. McNeill, trans. Ford Lewis Battles, Library of Christian Classics, vol. 1 (Philadelphia, Pa.: Westminster Press, 1960); 35, 37.

Tilda Norberg, *Ashes Transformed: Healing from Trauma* (Nashville, Tenn.: Upper Room Books, 2002), 71.

WEEK 8 CONTEMPLATIVE PRAYER

Thomas Ward, "Openness to All," *Weavings* (Jul/Aug 1996): 25.

Marjorie J. Thompson, "Wasting Time with God," *Weavings* (Mar/April 1989): 32.

Douglas V. Steere, *Dimensions of Prayer: Cultivating a Relationship with God*, rev. ed. (Nashville, Tenn.: Upper Room Books, 1997), 13.

Russell Maltby, *Obiter Scripta* (London: Epworth, 1952), 91.

Evelyn Underhill, "Breathing the Air of Eternity," *Weavings* (May/June 2002): 8.

WEEK 9 PRAYING WITH AND FOR OTHERS

Roberta C. Bondi, "The Paradox of Prayer," *Weavings* (Mar/Apr 1989): 9.

Wolpert, *Creating a Life with God*, 160.

Ibid., 162.

Marjorie J. Thompson, *Soul Feast: An Invitation to the Christian Spiritual Life* (Westminster/John Knox Press, 2005), 110.

Ann and Barry Ulanov, *Primary Speech: A Psychology of Prayer* (Louisville, Ky.: John Knox Press, 1982), 96.

Kristen Johnson Ingram, "Doing Prayer," *Weavings* (May/June 2002): 29.

WEEK 10 PRAYER AND SOCIAL TRANSFORMATION

Margaret Guenther, *The Practice of Prayer* (Boston: Cowley Publications, 1998), 5.

Douglas V. Steere, "Intercession: Caring for Souls," *Weavings* (Mar/Apr 1989): 25.

Wolpert, *Creating a Life with God*, 18.

Elizabeth J. Canham, *Journaling with Jeremiah* (Mahwah, N.J.: Paulist Press, 1992), 89.

Roberta C. Bondi, "The Paradox of Prayer," *Weavings* (Mar/Apr 1989): 15.

Evelyn Underhill, "Breathing the Air of Eternity," *Weavings* (May/June 2002): 7.

Resource List

The following list contains information about the Companions in Christ series, books that may be excerpted from in *The Way of Prayer* and resources that expand on the material in this book. As you read and share with your group, you may find some material that particularly challenges or helps you. To pursue individual reading on your own or if your small group wishes to follow up with additional resources, this list may be useful. Unless otherwise indicated, these books can be ordered at www.upperroom.org/bookstore/ or by calling 1-800-972-0433.

THE COMPANIONS IN CHRIST SERIES

Companions in Christ: A Small-Group Experience in Spiritual Formation (Participant's Book, #0914) by Gerrit Scott Dawson, Adele J. Gonzalez, E. Glenn Hinson, Rueben P. Job, Marjorie J. Thompson, and Wendy M. Wright

Companions in Christ: A Small-Group Experience in Spiritual Formation (Leader's Guide, #0915)by Stephen D. Bryant, Janice T. Grana, and Marjorie J. Thompson

The Way of Grace (Participant's Book, #9878) by John Indermark; Leader's Guide #9879 by Marjorie J. Thompson and Melissa Tidwell

The Way of Blessedness (Participant's Book, #0992) by Marjorie J. Thompson and Stephen D. Bryant; Leader's Guide #0994 by Stephen D. Bryant

The Way of Forgiveness (Participant's Book, #0980) by Marjorie J. Thompson; Leader's Guide #0981 by Stephen D. Bryant and Marjorie J. Thompson

The Way of Transforming Discipleship (Participant's Book, #9842) by Trevor Hudson and Stephen D. Bryant; Leader's Guide #9841 by Stephen D. Bryant

Exploring the Way: An Introduction to the Spiritual Journey (Participant's Book, #9806) by Marjorie J. Thompson; Leader's Guide #9807 by Marjorie J. Thompson and Stephen D. Bryant

The Way of the Child by Wynn McGregor

Leader's Guide and Sessions #9824
Family Booklet #9839
Resource Booklet #9825
Music CD #9845
Training DVD #9846
Church Pack #9847

The Way of the Child focuses on the spiritual formation of children ages 6–11. Part of the *Companions in Christ* series, it helps children learn and experience spiritual practices that will lead them into a deeper awareness of God's presence in their lives. The Leader's Guide includes five chapters on the spiritual nature of children and theory of faith formation as well as thirty-nine sessions to use with groups of children. There are enough sessions to use from September through May in Sunday school or weekday or weeknight settings. It is also designed for short-term use such as during Advent, Lent, or other special times of the year.

Journal: A Companion for Your Quiet Time
Introduction by Anne Broyles
Generous space for writing, faint lines to guide your journaling, and a layflat binding. Many pages contain inspirational thoughts to encourage your time of reflection.

Other Resources of Interest

The Upper Room Dictionary of Christian Spiritual Formation
by Keith Beasley-Topliffe
Nearly five hundred articles cover the people, methods, and concepts associated with spiritual formation with a primary emphasis on prayer and other spiritual disciplines. #0993

Alive Now
With a mix of prayers, award-winning poetry, stories of personal experience, and contributions from well-known authors, *Alive Now* offers readers a fresh perspective on living faithfully. Available as an individual subscription or group order.

Weavings: A Journal of the Christian Spiritual Life
Through thoughtful exploration of enduring spiritual life themes, *Weavings* offers trustworthy guidance on the journey to greater love for God and neighbor.

Week 1: How Do You Pray?

Maxie Dunnam, *The Workbook of Living Prayer* (Nashville, Tenn.: Upper Room Books, 1994).

John Indermark, *Traveling the Prayer Paths of Jesus* (Nashville, Tenn.: Upper Room Books, 2003); small-group Bible study.

Rueben P. Job and Norman Shawchuck, *A Guide to Prayer for All Who Seek God* (Nashville, Tenn.: Upper Room Books, 2006).

Larry James Peacock, *Openings: A Daybook of Saints, Psalms, and Prayer* (Nashville, Tenn.: Upper Room Books, 2003). Individuals learn and practice a new form of prayer each month; also has great God images.

Douglas V. Steere, *Dimensions of Prayer: Cultivating a Relationship with God* (Nashville, Tenn.: Upper Room Books, 1997).

Week 2: Images of God

Karla Kincannon, *Creativity and Divine Surprise: Finding the Place of Your Resurrection* (Nashville, Tenn.: Upper Room Books, 2005).

See Larry Peacock, *Openings* above and *Upper Room Worshipbook* below

Martha G. Rowlett, *Responding to God: A Guide to Daily Prayer* (Nashville, Tenn.: Upper Room Books, 1996).

Week 3: Praying by Heart

The Way of a Pilgrim, fwd. Walter J. Ciszek, trans. Helen Bacovcin (New York: Image Books, 1978).

Paul W. Chilcote, *Praying in the Wesleyan Spirit: 52 Prayers for Today* (Nashville, Tenn.: Upper Room Books, 2001).

Mary Lou Redding, *The Power of a Focused Heart: 8 Life Lessons from the Beatitudes* (Nashville, Tenn.: Upper Room Books, 2006).

Irma Zaleski, *Living the Jesus Prayer* (New York: Continuum, 1998).

Week 4: Praying with Music

Elise S. Eslinger, *The Upper Room Worshipbook,* revised (Nashville, Tenn.: Upper Room Books, 2006).

Beth A. Richardson, *Child of the Light: Walking through Advent and Christmas* (Nashville, Tenn.: Upper Room Books, 2005).

Week 5: Praying by Gaze

Elizabeth J. Canham, *A Table of Delight: Feasting with God in the Wilderness* (Nashville, Tenn.: Upper Room Books, 2005); individual or small groups.

J. Marshall Jenkins, *A Wakeful Faith: Spiritual Practice in the Real World* (Nashville, Tenn.: Upper Room Books, 2000); individuals.

W. Paul Jones, *An Eclectic Almanac for the Faithful: People, Places, and Events That Shape Us* (Nashville, Tenn.: Upper Room Books, 2006).

Henri J. M. Nouwen, *Behold the Beauty of the Lord* (Notre Dame, Ind.: Ave Maria Press, 1987).

Week 6: Praying with Our Bodies

James B. Nelson, *Embodiment: An Approach to Sexuality and Christian Theology* (Minneapolis, Minn.: Augsburg Fortress Publishers, 2003).

Jan Phillips, *Divining the Body: Reclaim the Holiness of Your Physical Self* (Woodstock, Vt.: SkyLight Paths Publishing, 2005).

Jane E. Vennard, *Praying with Body and Soul: A Way to Intimacy with God* (Minneapolis, Minn.: Augsburg Fortress Publishers, 1998).

Flora Slosson Wuellner, *Prayer and Our Bodies* (Nashville, Tenn.: Upper Room Books, 1987).

Week 7: Scriptural Prayer

Carolyn Stahl Bohler, *Opening to God: Guided Imagery Meditation on Scripture* (Nashville, Tenn.: Upper Room Books, 1996).

Elizabeth J. Canham, *Heart Whispers: Benedictine Wisdom for Today* (Nashville, Tenn.: Upper Room Books, 1999).

Thelma Hall, *Too Deep for Words: Rediscovering Lectio Divina* (New York: Paulist Press, 1988).

M. Robert Mulholland Jr., *Shaped by the Word: The Power of Scripture in Spiritual Formation,* rev. ed. (Nashville, Tenn.: Upper Room Books, 2001).

Norvene Vest, *Gathered in the Word: Praying the Scripture in Small Groups* (Nashville, Tenn.: Upper Room Books, 1997).

Ray Waddle, *A Turbulent Peace: The Psalms for Our Time* (Nashville, Tenn.: Upper Room Books, 2004); individuals.

WEEK 8: CONTEMPLATIVE PRAYER

Thomas Keating, *Open Mind, Open Heart*, 20th Anniversary Edition (New York: Continuum International Publishing Group, 2006).

J. David Muyskens, *Forty Days to a Closer Walk with God: The Practice of Centering Prayer* (Nashville, Tenn.: Upper Room Books, 2006).

Daniel Wolpert, *Creating a Life with God: The Call of Ancient Prayer Practices* (Nashville, Tenn.: Upper Room Books, 2003).

"Contemplative Life," *Weavings* (July/August 1992).

WEEK 9: PRAYING WITH AND FOR OTHERS

Michel Bouttier, *Prayers for My Village,* trans. Lamar Williamson (Nashville: Tenn.: Upper Room Books, 1994).

Maxie Dunnam, *The Workbook of Intercessory Prayer* (Nashville, Tenn.: Upper Room Books, 1989).

Danny E. Morris, Charles M. Olsen, *Discerning God's Will Together: A Spiritual Practice for the Church* (Nashville, Tenn.: Upper Room Books, 1997).

Tilda Norberg and Robert D. Webber, *Stretch Out Your Hand: Exploring Healing Prayer* (Nashville, Tenn.: Upper Room Books, 1998).

Martha Graybeal Rowlett, *Praying Together: Forming Prayer Ministries in Your Congregation* (Nashville, Tenn.: Upper Room Books, 2002).

Douglas V. Steere, *Dimensions of Prayer: Cultivating a Relationship with God* (Nashville, Tenn.: Upper Room Books, 1997).

Jane Vennard, *A Praying Congregation: The Art of Teaching Spiritual Practice* (Herndon, Va.: The Alban Institute, 2005).

WEEK 10: PRAYER AND SOCIAL TRANSFORMATION

Elizabeth J. Canham, *A Table of Delight: Feasting with God in the Wilderness* (Nashville, Tenn.: Upper Room Books, 2005).

Paul W. Chilcote, *Changed from Glory into Glory: Wesleyan Prayer for Transformation* (Nashville, Tenn.: Upper Room Books, 2005).

Gregory S. Clapper, *When the World Breaks Your Heart: Spiritual Ways of Living with Tragedy* (Nashville, Tenn.: Upper Room Books, 1999).

Kenda Creasy Dean and Ron Foster, *The Godbearing Life: The Art of Soul Tending for Youth Ministry* (Nashville, Tenn.: Upper Room Books, 1998).

GENERAL BOOKS ON PRAYER

Dorothy C. Bass and Don C. Richter, eds., *Way to Live: Christian Practices for Teens* (Nashville, Tenn.: Upper Room Books, 2002).

Steve Harper, *Devotional Life in the Wesleyan Tradition* (Nashville, Tenn.: Upper Room Books, 1995).

Wendy Miller, *Invitation to Presence: A Guide to Spiritual Disciplines* (Nashville, Tenn.: Upper Room Books, 1995).

Robert C. Morris, *Wrestling with Grace: A Spirituality for the Rough Edges of Life* (Nashville, Tenn.: Upper Room Books, 2003).

Marjorie Thompson, *Soul Feast: An Invitation to the Christian Spiritual Life* (Westminster/John Knox Press, 1995, 2005)

Daniel Wolpert, *Leading a Life with God: The Practice of Spiritual Leadership* (Nashville, Tenn.: Upper Room Books, 2006).

About the Authors

Jane E. Vennard, a United Church of Christ pastor, is Senior Adjunct Faculty of prayer and spirituality at the Iliff School of Theology in Denver. She is also a spiritual director, retreat leader, and the author of numerous articles and five books, the most recent of which is *A Praying Congregation: The Art of Teaching Spiritual Practice* (Alban Institute, 2005).

Stephen D. Bryant is editor and publisher of Upper Room Ministries. His vision of small groups as important settings for spiritual formation and his experience in the contemplative life as well as in local churches provided the inspiration for the *Companions in Christ* series. He is an ordained minister and former pastor in The United Methodist Church.

A most striking icon of the Lord Jesus Christ from 1670 made in the Armory School Moscow, which was started and headed by the famous and influential Russian iconographer Simon Ushakov. The term *Pantocrator* is Greek and means "the Ruler of All," for Christ is set to rule over all of heaven and earth (Acts 7:49).

"The Pantocrator," image compliments of St. Isaac of Syria Skete